Cover Design: Mulberry Marketing Communications

Interior Design: Mulberry Marketing Communications

Published by the ISSA Hygieia Network, Northbrook, Illinois, USA

Published simultaneously in Canada.

For information about special discounts available for bulk purchases or sales promotions contact:
The ISSA Hygieia Network,
3300 Dundee Road, Northbrook, IL 60062.
Tel.: 800-225-4772 (North America) or 847-982-0800.
www.hygieianetwork.org

First edition

ISBN: 978-X-XX-XXXXXX-X

Printed in the United States of America.

ISSA°
HYGIEIA
NETWORK

THE ISSA HYGIEIA NETWORK

Named after the Greek goddess of cleaning and hygiene, the ISSA Hygieia Network is an international community dedicated to the advancement and retention of women in all branches and at all levels of the global cleaning industry, with a special focus on cleaners' advancement.

With an overarching remit of supporting career advancement for women at all levels in the industry, the ISSA Hygieia Network undertakes activities that promote the entry into, advancement, and retention of women in the cleaning & hygiene industries.

The ISSA Hygieia Network also develops programs to reduce illiteracy levels and foster academic achievement in members, as well as campaign for the improvement of working conditions for immigrants and undeclared labor. Help is also offered to educate women on more personal topics such as healthy eating, childcare and health issues.

These objectives are met through a variety of initiatives including women's executive roundtables, the organization of a global awards scheme and receptions at major exhibitions and conferences to provide a supportive touchpoint for members and encourage the cross-fertilization of best practice ideas.

Be a part of the ISSA Hygieia Network and commit to securing a future, where all women and men in the cleaning industry are equally empowered and rewarded.

This vibrant, world-wide community is open to any woman or man employed in, or associated with, the cleaning industry. Both corporate and individual memberships are available.

ISSA Hygieia Network,
3300 Dundee Road, Northbrook, IL 60062 US
+1 800.225.4772
+1 847.982.0800

hygieianetwork.org

ACKNOWLEDGEMENTS

When writing such a wide-ranging and ambitious book about the essential, life-enhancing work that is undertaken by the often-invisible heroes of the cleaning industry, the acknowledgements necessary to thank and credit everyone could be a book in itself.

However, there are certain people who must be recognized for their part in turning my concept for an inspirational book into a published reality – without them, this book would not exist.

First, I would like to thank Andi Curry, the writer of these stories, who has so sensitively and movingly captured the amazing life stories that you will read here.

Secondly, I would like to thank Rafael Echevarria, VP of Corporate Communications at Diversey, for the original creative idea and the general management of the whole project. Together with Chris Klopper of Mulberry, they have lived and breathed this project for almost one year, and overseen its production at every stage.

The striking illustrations used are primarily the work of the talented Alicia Malesani and also Madli Silm while the evocative images reproduced are by renown Marseille-based photographer Philippe du Crest. The book's cover and internal design is by Lizzie Spencer at Mulberry Marketing Communications while her colleague Alex Weiss also deserves plaudits for undertaking many of the small, thankless but vital tasks associated with bringing a book to publication.

Mention too must be made of the inspiration that we continue to draw from Deborah Gillis and all at Catalyst. From them, I have learnt so much in our journey to advancing and educating the women of the cleaning industry.

I would like to acknowledge the support given by our friends at ISSA who have provided a welcome "home" for The Hygieia Network™. From the founding conversations and the first Governance document written together with John Garfinkel - Emeritus Executive Director of ISSA, to the latest financial contribution granted by the ISSA foundation; supported by Allen Soden – Chairman of the ISSA Foundation -, Richard Rones – ISSA president and President Americo- and finally John Barrett, Executive Director of ISSA who has been a fan and supporter from day one.

I would also like to honor the memory of my grandmother – my first role model, a cleaner and truly an invisible hero. She inspired me to look for the 'third door' and make this manifesto a reality and a reference in our industry today.

But more than anything, I am specially grateful and honored to share this amazing journey with an outstanding group of women: The ISSA Hygieia Network Council – Holly Borrego, Nathalie Doobin, Meredith Reuben, Linda Silverman, and Lydia Work. I am extremely appreciative of the inspiration, dedication and wise counsel that they freely give all of us in this industry. I would have never dreamt of meeting such a talented and passionate group of women, but if I had... they have clearly surpassed my dreams.

Dr. Ilham Kadri
Chairwoman
ISSA Hygieia Network

FOREWORD

Growing up in a modest home alongside a dirt road in rural Nova Scotia, the terms "diversity" and "inclusion" weren't commonly used in our community's dialogue. My parents had very little in terms of formal education or steady work, so the expectations for my future never went beyond the same limitations they faced in their own lives. The message they reinforced was clear: that success was a "good job" and steady income. This wasn't uncommon for young people in my town where career ambitions were often secondary to the practical realities of supporting a family.

But as my awareness of the world around me grew, it didn't take long for me to see the disparity between men and women in the workforce—a disparity that still exists today. Inspired by a group of women who successfully advocated to have gender equality rights included in the Canadian constitution, I decided to debate the topic in high school. My argument was titled: "Be it resolved that women earn the same as men." As I explored the subject, a fire was lit inside me that continues to burn through today.

While I understood the value of education and hard work, it became apparent in my postsecondary studies that I would never achieve career success based on merit alone. The first from my family to go to college, I found a purpose in advocating for equal opportunities for everyone. But I began to see that if I truly wanted to influence change and grow into an executive-level position, I would have to surround myself with people who believed in me. People who would not only serve as my mentors, but as role models and sponsors who would help me realize my full potential. People whose endorsement empowered me and gave me confidence despite my unconventional background. People who also welcomed me, spoke up for me and cleared a path for my future success.

Now, as the President & CEO of Catalyst, the leading nonprofit organization accelerating progress for women through workplace inclusion, I am fortunate to work with the top companies and business leaders throughout the world that are looking to change workplaces, society and lives for the better.

Not all women have people in their corner as I did; in fact, most do not. Essentially, there's been very little progress in the C-Suite for the last two generations of women: from 1955-2017, only 62 individual women have served or are currently serving as CEOs of a Fortune 500 company. And women's representation in boardrooms across the globe is dismal. Progress this slow is not progress at all.

But the issue goes beyond representation—women must also work harder and longer to earn the wages of their male counterparts. Pew Research Center data shows it would take women an additional 44 days of work to earn the same as males in their position. Black women face an even larger disparity in pay: Research from the National Women's Law Center finds that Black women earn $0.63 for every dollar earned by white men.

Men continue to dominate many industries, including the professional cleaning industry. It's not uncommon to see women and people of color working in frontline custodial positions, but the numbers become fewer the higher in the ranks you look. This issue is familiar to me—growing up, my mother worked as a housekeeper; my sisters cleaning hotel rooms.

That's why the work of the Hygieia Network and the profiles you'll read in this book are so important. The pages of this book are filled with stories of inspiration, challenge, persistence and grit—stories of several incredible individuals who have worked despite the odds to show up—for their

businesses, their families and their communities.

While we need more role models to inspire young women and show them potential pathways for success, this book isn't just for women. It is also for men who are looking to influence cultural and organizational change. Men who see the opportunity that exists when you have a truly diverse and inclusive team of leaders driving the business. Men who choose to sponsor a woman or a woman of color. Because as our research shows, embracing cultures of inclusion and diversity are not only the right thing to do, it is a smart way to improve business results.

At Catalyst, we like to say that diversity is a fact and inclusion is a choice. It is my sincere hope that this book inspires you to make a choice for more inclusive workplaces.

Deborah Gillis
President & CEO
Catalyst

Dr. Ilham Kadri

While Dr. Ilham Kadri grew up lacking basic essentials such as quality food, electricity and running water, her illiterate grandmother made sure she grew up with love and regularly impressed the importance of education. Dr. Kadri's inspirational story shows how hard work, knowledge and perseverance can make dreams reality.

Name:
Dr. Ilham Kadri

Title:
President & CEO

Company:
Diversey

About the Business:
Diversey is the leading provider of smart, sustainable solutions for cleaning and hygiene, driving increased productivity, food safety and infection prevention. Diversey offers chemicals, floor care machines, tools and equipment, plus a wide range of technology based value-added services, food safety services as well as water and energy management solutions that ultimately enhance customers' end user experience. The company serves customers in more than 175 countries in the building management, hospitality, food service, retail, health care, education and government sectors.

Her Current Home:
Charlotte, North Carolina

Her First Book:
Ilham's school awarded perfectly performing students with books at the end of the school year. Her first book was Cinderella.

One of her proudest achievements:
Founding the Hygieia Network™, an organization aimed at combating illiteracy and advancing the roles of women at all levels in the cleaning and hygiene industry's workforce.

"I was extremely lucky to have my grandmother in my life, because I grew up in a place filled with a lot of love. She was extremely dedicated to helping me achieve more through education and knowledge."

Not until many years later did she stop to reflect on everything that had happened. She walked alongside her husband at Souk, a busy bazaar in Essaouira, Morocco. The two meandered slowly between the colorful stalls filled with elaborate textiles, exotic spices and foods when two young girls passed them. The girls wore cheap, tattered and discolored school uniforms and their sandals were to the point of deterioration that only a few threads separated their feet from the dirt.

"You see those girls there," she pointed. "That was me when I was little."

Her husband turned to her, his face filled with benevolent surprise.

"Ilham," he responded, slightly shaking his head. "Do you realize how much you've accomplished in your amazing journey?"

She spent the rest of the day reflecting on his words. It had been several years since she'd walked the streets of Morocco with little other than a book and the clothes on her back. Today she was President and CEO of a multi-billion dollar global business, had a Ph.D. and was the recipient of numerous leadership awards. She'd earned wide recognition as "the water lady" in the Middle East, sat on the board of directors for a Fortune 500 company and founded an organization supporting literacy efforts in the cleaning industry in memory of her illiterate grandmother. She enjoyed a happy marriage and was mother to a young son. He was right, she concluded. She had come a long way.

...

Dr. Ilham Kadri is President and CEO of Diversey, a $2.6 billion global provider of smart and sustainable solutions for cleaning and hygiene. She says that during her life, she has been gifted many lives—lives that have taken her to residences in 13 cities across five continents since she left her childhood home in Casablanca, Morocco, at age 17.

While the thought of Casablanca evokes images of Hollywood glamour due to the popular movie of that name filmed in the early 1940s, Ilham's early experiences were far from the bright lights. Her name means "inspiration" in Arabic and her grandmother once told her that it didn't matter if she was successful or rich, but that she must always be inspired and continue learning, unlearning and relearning.

Raised by her grandmother in a small, one-room building, Ilham had very little growing up. In fact, she had just two toys—a doll and a teddy bear. There were many nights she went to bed hungry because there wasn't enough money for food. Her grandmother was illiterate, which was common for many Arab women during that time, and worked as a cleaner for a prominent French family. While the work was regular, she earned a pittance as there were no wage laws established in Morocco then.

Ilham, aged 9, at home in Casablanca

Though they had no electricity, running water and only the barest of essentials, Ilham says that she never felt deprived because there was so much love in their home. She spent many days occupying her own time while her grandmother worked, and used her imagination to create new worlds that lay beyond the walls of her home. As she grew older, she started reading— television wasn't an option and music was too expensive to pursue, so she eagerly devoured every book she could get her hands on to fill the long days.

"I was extremely lucky to have my grandmother in my life, because I grew up in a place filled with a lot of love," she said. "She was extremely dedicated to helping me achieve more through education and knowledge."

Her grandmother regularly told her that when you were a little girl in Morocco, you had two exits: one that led from your father's home to your husband's house, and one that led to your grave. She regularly challenged Ilham to find her third exit, which was through education and knowledge.

But finding that third exit wasn't easy for Ilham. When it came time to attend school, she faced an uphill battle. She struggled with communication—her brain would think so quickly that she was unable to process the thoughts into words fast enough to speak and contribute to conversations. Teachers said she just wasn't smart, despite her grandmother's insistence to the contrary. Eventually Ilham became so frustrated that she began to withdraw from social settings and kept mostly to herself while other kids played around her. She changed schools more than once to resolve the issue, but it wasn't until she was 13 years old that teachers finally realized Ilham had dyslexia.

With the encouragement of her grandmother and skills she adapted to navigate her learning disability, Ilham eventually began thriving in school. She was recognized for her aptitude and intellect, with teachers promising her a great future if she continued along her current path. But just prior to her high school graduation, she experienced another setback when she contracted typhoid fever from drinking contaminated water. Bedridden in a hospital for several months, her recovery was uncertain. Slowly, she gained strength and was eventually nurtured back to health. It was an experience she would never forget and would later develop into a personal cause.

"It was tough," Ilham recalled. "I lost a lot of weight, and all of my long, black hair fell out. But my grandmother was fabulous along with our neighbors and local community members. My friends would bring me my courses and I would train alone when I could. It was a miracle, but I passed the final exam that allowed me to graduate with a scholarship to one of the elite schools in France."

DEFYING GENDER STEREOTYPES

From the moment she stepped out of her childhood home to continue her education in college, Ilham took her grandmother's words to heart, aggressively navigating a journey to find her third exit out of Morocco through knowledge. Refusing to yield when frustrations or conventional gender barriers were thrown in her way, she embraced a future in mechanical engineering.

Across the region, her potential was widely recognized. Ilham was accepted into the most prestigious programs and lauded for her research. She studied relentlessly, often

spending 12 to 16 hours in the labs each day. The further she got into her education, the more of an anomaly she became. She was often the only woman in the labs where she worked, which Ilham says never was an issue for her. She just wanted to be the best she could in her own journey.

Her studies took her to France, Canada and then back to France where she went on to complete her doctorate in physics and chemistry. She was highly sought-after by recruiters and large corporations and received several job offers before even completing her thesis. She ultimately accepted a position with Shell, the Dutch Petroleum Company.

Early on, an aptitude test identified her leadership abilities but she had so little exposure to anything beyond the lab that imagining herself as anything but a chemist seemed laughable.

"I remember hearing that and for me it was like science fiction," she said. "How would they tell me how I was going to end my career? And frankly at that point, I really didn't care."

Her first team at Shell consisted of two other people—quite a departure from the global team of 11,000 employees she manages today. The team invented and patented the first plastic wine cork, which earned her wide recognition throughout the company. With all eyes on her, Ilham embraced the resources extended to her through Shell's leadership program and continued persevering in a very much male-dominated environment.

To climb the corporate ladder, she took on various roles within the company so she could learn the business from all sides. Before long, she was negotiating large automotive deals with Renault, Peugeot-Citroen, Toyota and the like, which further distanced her from other career paths which are typically dominated by women.

"I remember going to customers in Japan or Germany with my technical leader who was also a woman, and telling them we'd fix their paint problems in the body shop," she said. "They looked at us so strangely, like they couldn't believe two women could possibly know how to paint an automobile."

As much as she blazed the trail for young females in the industry, her success hasn't come without challenges. Threatened colleagues tried to intimidate her more than once, and she says there were times when she potentially risked her career by refusing to back down when opposed by people who thought she was too young or who did not respect her strong-minded views on how to disrupt the status quo. Ultimately, she never gave in and now makes a concerted effort to develop workplace environments that are supportive of diversity and inclusion and channels for people to report harassment. Those same channels helped her climb to where she is today.

"I'm passionate about diversity because I'm the pure product of diversity and inclusion," she said. "From my days as little girl with limited resources and barely enough money to buy a dress to wear to school to where I am now—if I didn't have people around me who have given me a chance, mentored me, coached me, included me in the community and working environment, I wouldn't have made it."

LEFT BEHIND AND MOVING AHEAD

Once Ilham left Shell, she took on several new positions that strengthened her corporate leadership experience. But when she married and gave birth to her first child, things changed and priorities shifted.

During her pregnancy, she was co-leading a merger and acquisition team in the sale of a division of her organization and traveled extensively to locations throughout Korea, China, Japan and Malaysia. Despite her leading role in the sale, Ilham turned her focus on her family and her new role as a mother once her son was born. She was determined to spend her full maternity leave bonding with him. But she found that when she returned to work four months later, the company had forged ahead without her.

"I was always ambitious and wanted to accomplish more, but there was this misconception that I would return from maternity leave and not want to travel or dedicate myself to my work anymore," she said.

It was at that point that Ilham realized she wasn't in the right environment. She liked her job, but felt the culture didn't align with her values and goals. She

ILHAM'S RECIPE FOR SUCCESS

When I reflect on my own recipe for success in leadership roles, I realize that I always focus on the journey rather than the destination. Throughout my journey, I have used the following ingredients that I nurtured along the way:

1. **Passion is my driver**
   I am effective when I love what I do and when I am inspired by other leaders who allow me to use my expertise and intuition to make sound business decisions, including thinking and acting outside the traditional defined corporate box.
   I always found that if my passion was not there, my path would undeniably change.

2. **Curiosity is my engine**
   My illiterate grandmother, who educated me, taught me to love books, respect knowledge and admire the people who expressed their ideas in print. Some of these people became my role models.

3. **Humility as a top attribute**
   I consider this the secret attribute of great leaders. Being both an African and an Arab leader, I learned to listen to the wisdom of others and to know and understand my history before making a decision that shaped my future.

4. **Mentoring as a support**
   I was privileged to meet outstanding mentors, who allowed me to run the extra mile. From my professor in Strasbourg University who offered me the chance to be the first female working with a twin screw extruder in his lab, to the professor who convinced me to learn sales in the highly male-predominant automotive area, to my current CEO who appointed me as the first female and Arab leader of the division's Middle East and Africa region.

5. **Determination and resilience as survival tools**
   Without these attributes, I would have changed my path several times, but at the expense of my dreams.

6. **Sense of purpose and taking ownership of my roles**
   At home, I am a wife and a mother. At work, I am a colleague and a leader. As a world citizen, I contribute to and defend my values while enjoying mentoring potential future leaders.

As a final thought, I firmly believe that culture matters. At the crossroads of the Arab and African worlds in which I was raised, our personal and professional journey is shaped by the social eco-system in which we live. I believe that behind every woman is a great mother or great grandmother, and a great father or a great husband. By mentoring young women, we can help shape their professional journey while respecting their own roots.

As published in Kerstin Plehwe's book "Female Leadership - DIE MACHT DER FRAUEN" came to the conclusion that in order to continue growing, she needed to leave.

She also knew that following her passion would require strong support and encouragement from her husband. They each had demanding professional roles, and with the arrival of their son, more was at stake. After much discussion, her husband made the decision to step back from his career to give the family more flexibility and allow him to be more hands-on with their son. He encouraged Ilham to follow her passions and dreams.

"My husband is my best fan and supporter," she said. "I am blessed to have a great man in my life—greater than me. Ultimately, I work best when I work with passion, when I love what I do. And this shows both at work and at home. Without him, I couldn't do what I do."

FUELING HER PASSION

Once Ilham made the decision to follow her passion, her career has continued to take off. She's committed herself to causes that are close to her, including clean water, sustainability, fighting illiteracy, and elevating the profiles of cleaning workers, like her grandmother.

When she accepted a position with an organization that was later acquired by Dow, she became the first woman to lead expansion efforts throughout the Middle East and Africa. In this role, she negotiated strategic water projects in the Kingdom of Saudi Arabia focused on providing millions of people with unprecedented access to clean water through the use of the best sustainable technology available at that time - a cause close to her heart considering her own experience drinking contaminated water.

In 2013, she accepted a position as President of the Diversey Care Division of Sealed Air. She was excited by the opportunity as it gave her a chance to recognize her grandmother and give back to an industry that had provided for her during her childhood. Since she took the helm, Ilham has completely transformed the business, leading it through four consecutive years of double digit profitable growth by substantially increasing the engagement of its employees.

While her educational background was in chemistry and sciences, Ilham has developed a long and proven record of building teams and turning around businesses. She works with passion, and inspires everyone around her to work to their full potential. She's a change agent, not only changing the course of the businesses she leads, but also disrupting the behavior of entire industries through innovation and technology.

TOMORROW, IN THE BAZAAR

On that day in the bazaar, Ilham took careful stock of not just where she is, but the journey that got her to that destination. She thought about her grandmother and how she worked so hard to lay the foundation upon which Ilham would build her future. She considered teachers and academics who recognized her potential and helped her identify her passion for chemistry. She looked at her husband, who had walked alongside her for much of her professional career, encouraging her when she experienced doubt and challenging her to follow her passions and dreams.

She thought about the nature of her work and the impact she was making. She thought about the legacy she wanted to leave for future generations. She thought about the millions of people who would now have better access to clean water through clean energy because of her efforts, the cleaners who would learn how to read and the women who would go on to thrive in their careers due to the mentoring opportunities she had made available. She thought about her son and the model she was setting for him.

That day in the bazaar she stopped to think and reflect, but it wasn't for long. Because for Dr. Ilham Kadri, it's not about what's now, but what's next. And how she will get there.

Gemma Beylouny

From the slums of the Philippines to the suburbs of Atlanta, Gemma Beylouny has traveled far and seen a lot in her short years. As the proud owner of Rejoice Maids, she is a living testament to what dreams you can realize if you never give up.

As a young child growing up in the Philippines, Gemma Beylouny always wanted to be like Ms. Castillo. Ms. Castillo owned a garment factory that exported clothes to retailers in the U.S. She lived in a huge home with immaculate gardens that sat just beyond the gates separating the rich from the poor. She was married to a lawyer and wore fancy clothes, her hair always perfectly coiffed. To Gemma, Ms. Castillo seemed perfect in every way. As chauffeurs escorted Ms. Castillo around town, Gemma would sit along the side of the road, watching the big black car drive by the ghetto where Gemma lived with her mother and seven siblings. As Ms. Castillo passed, she stared blankly out the window of her car, looking past the filth of the streets.

Ms. Castillo didn't have to share one bathroom with 200 other people.
Ms. Castillo didn't have to eat chicken feet for dinner because she couldn't afford the thighs or breast.
Ms. Castillo didn't have to dig through trash to find books or worry about cockroaches crawling into her mouth when she slept.

That's why Gemma wanted to be Ms. Castillo.

Name:
Gemma Beylouny

Business:
Rejoice Maids

Location:
Woodstock, Georgia

No. of Employees:
20

Three Songs She Wants Played at Her Wake:
"Climb" by Miley Cyrus, to represent her journey to where she is now.

"Roar" by Katy Perry, because she refuses to sit quietly when she doesn't agree with something.

"My Way" by Frank Sinatra, because she likes to live life on her own terms.

Gemma says she was "lucky" growing up, because as the youngest child, she had seven older brothers and sisters who helped look out for her. Her mother worked long hours hand washing clothes. When she came home at night, her arms discolored from the water and detergent, hands shaking from pain, Gemma could hear her crying, but said that she never complained. She was angry, but she didn't complain.

It wasn't until Gemma reached adolescence that she realized her family was poor. For her, walking a mile to get to school was normal. But her passion for learning is what pushed her forward, despite her fourth-grade teacher telling her that she would "never amount to anything" and to "stay in the ghetto where you belong."

"I always liked to read and have an urge to learn," she said. "I am very curious about a lot of things."

Gemma says she was "not born with intelligence" and she credits her "grit" for getting her through hard times, but she was always looking for ways to learn, even as a young child. She spent hours on the streets outside friends' homes watching their little black and white televisions through the windows. It's how she learned to speak English. Most shows were in her native language of Tagalog, but the commercials were in a mix of Tagalog and English, so she began to understand the language contextually.

"When we moved to Manila, I wasn't going to school but I always looked for ways to read," she said. "Garbage cans were always outside the homes of the rich, and I'd dig through them to find new books. I love to read."

All of the children did what they could to earn money for food. Many of Gemma's siblings worked as houseboys or maids, where they cleaned, helped prepare meals or watched young children. Because of Gemma's high energy, her mother always pushed her away from the housekeeping duties and toward selling things on the street. She'd wake up with her mother at 4 a.m. on the weekends to shred yuca. Her mother cooked it and Gemma sold it in the streets.

But it wasn't until Gemma met her husband, George, much later in her life, that she was able to "break the cycle" and receive a formal education. She said it was George who inspired her to improve, become better and educate herself.

LEARNING CURVES

Once the two married and left the Philippines, their next stop was Guam. George was in the Navy and the newlyweds lived on the base. It was there that Gemma first tried to get her driver's license. In the Philippines, her family never had a car—she had never even been in a car as a child—so she felt that learning to drive would be a great accomplishment.

"I tried to learn to drive on a stick shift," she said, laughing. "The Guamanians or Chamorros just hated me. The first time, I fail and I kept crying. I kept trying. I fail again. It got to the point they would see me and run."

Gemma tested five times, but did not receive her license during the two years they lived in Guam. But she never gave up on her goal. When she came to the U.S., she continued practicing until the day she walked out of the Bureau of Motor Vehicles with her driver's license in hand. It was the first of a series of great accomplishments.

George and Gemma had two daughters and once they reached school age, Gemma's next goal was to earn her GED. Her formal education stopped after grade school, so she enrolled in a night program to earn her diploma. The days were long, as she spent all day cleaning houses and evenings attending classes. It took her about a year before she was ready to take the test. And the first two times she tested, she failed.

"The morning of Sept. 11, 2001, I received a call from the woman at the center," she said. "We talked about the planes a little before she told me I passed the test. I couldn't believe it, I was so excited. I was probably the only happy person on that day."

Immediately, she called the admissions department at Kennesaw State University, which is located in the northwestern suburbs of Atlanta. She took an assessment test and enrolled in their business program.

"Everything was so foreign to me and so much harder than my GED program," she said. "I think not having the foundation of going through the formal education to support me was so much more difficult. I had to take Calculus 1101 so many times I can't even remember."

With the help of professors who recognized the effort she was putting into it, she was able to work through the program. She cleaned houses during the day, then went to school in the evenings. The schedule was exhausting and at one point, the stress became so overwhelming, she got gum disease and became a borderline diabetic from not eating regularly or healthily.

It took her three times before she passed Finance 1101 and twice to pass economics, but she did it.

"For a lot of people, when you pass a class it's just normal," she said. "But for me, it was a really big deal. It's a super reward. It was hard, but I never once considered quitting."

After five years without a single break (including summers), Gemma graduated with a bachelor's degree in business administration.

FROM A HOME CLEANER TO A HOME CLEANING BUSINESS

In 2010, Gemma launched her business, Rejoice Maids. She had spent the past several years cleaning homes, so she thought starting a residential cleaning business would be easy.

She discovered quickly that assumption was wrong.

"It was a nightmare. I didn't know how to train my employees, my clients," she said. "Every day, I hated going to my little teeny-weeny office. I don't know what I was thinking — I acted like I was still in the ghetto. It was like, 'Hey, you clean this and I'll pay you and we're good.' It just wasn't that way."

Feeling like she had a bullseye on her forehead after being sued by former employees for false claims, Gemma looked for resources that would help her better manage the business. She wanted to put protocols in place and set up programs for managing her staff. Similarly, she needed to develop tools to communicate better with her clients and set expectations.

That's when she found the Association of Residential Cleaning Services International (ARCSI). Through the association, she networked with other members who shared strategies they found effective in running their own businesses. The group has offered great camaraderie that has given her strength through the tough times.

"By talking to [other ARCSI members], you know you're not alone anymore," she said. "There are people just like you trying to survive and make it better. It did help a lot."

With better processes in place and a great network of people to whom she can turn when she has a problem or question, Gemma has steadily grown Rejoice Maids. She now has 20 employees and services Cherokee County and parts of neighboring counties just outside Atlanta. She advertises her business through print and online advertising, and is working to expand her reach.

One of her proudest achievements is the recent purchase of a two-story, 8,200-square-foot office building that is located at the corner of a busy intersection. She operates the business from the first floor and rents out the second floor to several other businesses.

"You hear a lot of stories of how people don't manage their house cleaning businesses well," she said. "They might have 50 employees, but they aren't making any money. It took me a long time to figure out I was doing it the wrong way, but now I know. I'm still learning every day. I became better."

MAKING IT BETTER

Even as a young girl sleeping on the dirt floor of her family's shack, Gemma Beylouny knew one day she would reach her goal. She didn't know how it would happen, but

Ms. Castillo made such an impression on Gemma that later in life, she tried adopting her image. She cut her long, dark brown hair and tried to dye it blondish brown like Ms. Castillo. But her plan backfired, and her hair turned purple.

"People said I looked like Jackie Chan, but I thought I looked more like Bruce Lee," she said, laughing. "I look much better as me."

she just knew she would do it. And she has. She's fought through extreme adversity and challenge with grit and determination. She hasn't given up. She doesn't complain. She just keeps going.

Gemma said that knowing what it's like to be poor is what keeps her going.

"I don't ever want to be poor again, being poor is so hard. People look at you like you're nothing. You don't count in the world, it's like you don't exist."

Now that she's gotten to a place where she can help others, Gemma is focused on paying it forward. As a child, she benefitted from the generous assistance of civic organizations such as the Rotary and Kiwanis, so she works in these groups to help other families in need. She is a charter member of her local Rotary.

Wanting to help out other families like hers in the Philippines, she works through local charities to donate meals. In 2015, Rejoice Maids provided meals for 20 families in the Philippines; in 2016, 60 families received meals. Rejoice Maids also provided 60 children with school supplies last year. As she continues to grow her business, Gemma aims to feed as many as 100,000 people over the next 15 years.

In 2016, she started the Rejoice Foundation to encourage fellow business owners to contribute to improving the lives of people in her local community. One program she's helped launch is Must Ministry's Summer Lunch Program that makes sure school-aged children have access to nutritious lunches when school isn't in session. The program is in its fourth year and delivers lunches one day a week for the whole summer to deserving students throughout the area.

She wants to make it better for the people who work for her too. She knows what it's like to feel like a servant in someone else's home, and she never wants her employees to feel that way. She regularly serves them food and looks for ways to show them how much she appreciates them. She encourages them to take classes and learn more about the profession.

For Gemma, it's not about looking back but looking ahead.

"This is my opportunity to make things better," she said. "I knew during the times we were being treated wrong. But you've gotta move on and think of better things."

And move on, she has. Ms. Castillo would be so impressed.

Holly Borrego

When she started cleaning at night so she didn't have to send her young daughter to daycare, Holly Borrego never imagined she would stay in the industry, let alone make an extremely successful career out of it. In a job where everyone is always telling you what's wrong, Holly shares important advice on how focusing on what you can control can help you drown out the negativity and achieve success.

Name:
Holly Borrego

Title:
Senior Director of Cleaning Services

Company:
C&W Services

Location:
Kansas City, Missouri

Previous Jobs:
Bank teller

Mentors:
Ron Baker
one of the owners of the BG Service Solutions

Van Bedell
VP of Business Development

Best Advice She's Ever Received:
"I had a boss who once told me, that if I lived a lifestyle that could be supported by the money you would make flipping burgers, that I would have no stress. And I've lived by that. I could pay all of my bills on 25 percent of my income. It gives you a whole different level of freedom."

Advice to Other Women:

Don't be afraid to ask questions and learn as much as you can.

> "You need to be a great people person, but you also need to understand the science of cleaning. Most people are good at one of those things and not the other. If you can learn to balance those two things, you'll be successful."

The phone rang and Holly Borrego answered it.

"I'm having a bad day, so you're going to have a bad day," said the man on the other end of the line.

She quickly realized who it was—it wasn't the first time this customer had called to complain. He proceeded to tell her that someone had neglected to wipe down the hand rails in his building and he found dust on them. She acknowledged the situation and told him she would send someone over to dust the rails—knowing full well that there was no dust, he just wanted to complain.

Many contract cleaners have this type of conversation on a regular basis, and Holly Borrego is no different. Throughout her career, she has dealt with numerous difficult clients. She's been screamed at and told she's worthless. She's had a client who openly hated women and another who, despite evidence to the contrary, was so insistent that her team had damaged the walls in the building, that he sent her a $10,000 bill.

"I can't believe you'd even show your face around here," he told her when she came to address the charges.

It's a tough job that is not for everyone. Holly said that when she started, she was afraid of her own shadow. But several years of experience working with cleaners and clients alike have helped her realize that when someone yells at her, it's not her they are yelling at, but a representative of the company.

With the support of a few strong mentors and leaders who believed in her, Holly persevered when a lot of other women quit. She loves cleaning and has charted a successful career path by finding ways to standardize the way people clean and identifying smart solutions that make cleaning easier. This perseverance and dedication have led her to her current position as the Senior Director of Cleaning Services at C&W Services, a leading facilities services and management company that covers all of North America.

CLEANER TO A REGIONAL VICE PRESIDENT

Holly started her career cleaning office buildings at night for $3.35/hour. Working while her baby slept, the job gave her the ability to spend time with her daughter during the day and avoid daycare. Holly said she was like a lot of the other people cleaning buildings in the suburbs of Kansas City in the late '80s. The wages were low, but women liked the flexibility of the hours and the opportunity to get out of the house.

Holly loved her job and the assignment, but she didn't stay in the position for long. Promotions came quickly and frequently for the young mother who worked hard, demonstrated an attention to detail and simply "showed up," as she tells it.

In just a few years, Holly ascended through the ranks of the regional contract cleaning company, becoming the senior operations manager of a $25-million branch in Kansas City. She dedicated herself to learning every aspect of the business and identifying ways to make it more efficient—and the promotions followed. For example, she was tasked with workloading every building in the company's four territories to reduce labor costs. At the conclusion of the project, she achieved a two percent labor reduction and was promoted again.

Holly threw herself into the business, learning everything she could about how it worked and how she could increase efficiencies. Another important skill she picked up during this period was learning to speak Spanish.

"It's almost impossible not to learn Spanish when you're completely immersed in it 8-12 hours a day," she said. "I worked with the greatest people who drilled me on my pronunciation—they taught me like I was a two-year-old. I also bought a Spanish speaking series at a garage sale that helped me with the structure of the language."

Being bilingual made her an invaluable asset to her employer, which was one of the largest cleaning service providers in the area at that time. Not only could she converse with workers, she was also able to create training materials and operational programs.

"Our owners were great people, and they really prided themselves on quality service," she said. "It was a great environment to learn in."

Before her company was bought out in 2008, she was promoted to Regional Vice President and managed approximately $35 million to $40 million in cleaning business across Kansas and Missouri.

MAKING CLEANING BETTER

A key component to Holly's success is her focus on continual improvement. She is always looking for ways to make herself, the people on her team and the business she manages, better.

Much of what she's learned has been "trial by fire." She reads books, studies other managers and isn't afraid to ask questions when faced with a challenge. She earned her Bachelors of Business Administration degree in 2013, but said that she read more books about business in the years leading up to that than she ever did studying for her degree.

"I remember early in my career, my boss handed me a budget and said, 'Here you go, figure it out,'" she recalled. "I'd never even seen a budget before, so the first thing I had to do was figure out the components of a budget. I bought a book on basic accounting and another on budgeting. And I figured it out."

That's how she figured out how to use a computer, develop a business plan, create costing models and more. She was the first person in her department to get a computer, because she insisted it would help her better track and manage her teams. Within a short period, she taught herself Microsoft Office and Word and began developing spreadsheets and materials to track inventory, labor and bids, while also training her teams. The latter of which, was a key focus for her.

"Training is so important," she said. "I required every manager to train their frontline employees each quarter; they would have to turn in a signature sheet in order to get their bonus. We wanted to promote people from within, so a frontline cleaner who can't speak English can work their way up to a position where they are fluent in English, running their own territory and earning $90,000. That was the goal."

Just as she's focused on making herself and her teams better, she also wants to make the way people clean better. And faster.

"As a building supervisor, I oversaw the cleaning of a 16-story building," she said. "There were nights when I had eight floors without anyone on them. So I know what it's like to run when you're emptying trash.

And to vacuum until you have blisters on your hands. When you have experiences like that, you know there's got to be a better way."

One of her early initiatives was a training program called the "Power of Five," which she developed after analyzing complaints. She'd found that 75 percent of the complaints they received stemmed from the five most basic functions or responsibilities, like locking doors, turning off lights, stocking restrooms. Holly's training program included modules around each position, which reinforced best practices in these areas. For example, basic cleaners were given five basic responsibilities: pull trash, dust, clean the floor (mop or vacuum), turn out the lights and lock the doors. All of the training material supported each of the positions, from floor techs all the way up to area managers.

She recognizes that when cleaners have better training and tools, they go home less tired. She's seen the direct impact this has on productivity, retention and the value to the customer.

"It's not about making the cleaner go faster, it's really about doing the process better," she said. "If you concentrate on the health and well-being of the cleaner, out of that you'll get good results."

Highlighting that today's cleaning tools are not much different from the tools someone used to clean 100 years ago, Holly works closely with manufacturers to help develop new tools and technology that address inefficiencies and improve processes.

"You can't survive in a janitorial company making your cleaners go faster," she said. "Cleaning isn't consistent, turnover is high and you just end up trading accounts with your competitors. You need to find ways to make the cleaning better."

WHERE ARE THE WOMEN?

When she was in janitorial operations, Holly was a minority. Women filled customer service positions, but few made it for very long in the field. She was the only female out of 39 general managers.

She recalled an incident when she was attending a trade show with her procurement officer, who was a man. The two visited a booth and she posed a series of questions about the equipment to the salesperson in the booth. After each question, the salesperson responded to her companion, and refused to look at Holly directly.

"I got so frustrated I just walked away," she said. "My procurement guy told him how stupid it was, because he lost a lot of potential business by doing that."

She attributes the lack of female representation in operational positions to the fact that women just don't apply for those positions. "If you put an advertisement for an operations manager in the paper, 99 percent of the people who apply will be men," she said. "I can't remember the last time I had a woman apply for that job. Now if I listed it as an account manager, we could at least get women in the door."

She would like to see more women get involved, particularly in operations, but she suggests that women need to be able to have tough conversations, whether they are with cleaning workers or clients. It's also important that individuals in these positions not be overly sensitive.

"It can be such a negative industry," she said. "You're always told what you did wrong, and you're never told what you did right. You can empty 5,000 garbage cans, but if you missed one, you will hear about it. You just can't take it personally."

She has found that by focusing on how she can improve the service, she is able to avoid the personal feelings that might come into play.

"It's tough for a lot of people, because there are two completely different skill sets required to be successful in this industry," she said. "You need to be a great people person, but you also need to understand the science of cleaning. Most people are good at one of those things and not the other. If you can learn to balance those two things, you'll be successful."

RECIPE FOR SUCCESS

Holly Borrego has never liked boredom. That's why, she said, the cleaning industry has been such a great fit for her over the years.

"It's such a dynamic industry and it constantly challenges me," she said. "This is the only job I've ever had where it's impossible to be bored. From creating proposals to training plans, managing people and managing clients—there are so many moving parts, that it's impossible to be bored. I just love it."

And just as she's embraced the industry, it has also embraced her. She said she's "lucky" that she started her career working with cleaners before she had to manage clients, as that prepared her. While luck might play a small role, it's easy to see that Holly's hard work, resourcefulness and perseverance have played a large part in her success too.

Janelle Bruland

A little more than two decades ago, Janelle Bruland started her business from her living room. She has since built it into one of the largest contract cleaning companies in the Pacific Northwest. This entrepreneur, CEO and Immediate Past President of the Building Services Contractors Association International (BSCAI) offers insights into how decisiveness, dedicated time management principles and strong relationships throughout the industry and local community have helped fuel her success.

Name:
Janelle Bruland, CBSE

Company:
MSNW

Location:
Whatcom County, Washington

Where MSNW Operates:
Washington, Oregon and Idaho

No. of Employees:
Approximately 400

What She Does
When She's Stressed:
Her faith carries her through all she does, but you can also find her meditating or exercising if things are stressful

Janelle Bruland gathered her new team of 10 employees in her living room. Nine months pregnant with her second daughter, she had just purchased Management Services Northwest (now MSNW), a small contract cleaning company with a handful of accounts located in Whatcom County, Washington.

"I know little about the cleaning industry," she confessed to her team. "But I do know something about business. I'm hoping we can work together and you can help teach me."

Recognizing that strong relationships were the foundation of a successful business, Janelle made a commitment that she would work closely with her team and provide the resources they needed to take excellent care of their accounts.

"When our customers are happy, they will refer us to other businesses and we'll grow," she told them.

And that's exactly what happened. With the slogan "We'll take care of it," Janelle Bruland and her team are not only taking great care of their customers, but their local community as well.

Situated in the northwestern-most corner of the continental U.S., Whatcom County, Washington, has a picturesque landscape that features the beauty of the Cascade Mountain range and the Pacific coastline. It's where Janelle Bruland has lived her entire life and the place where she started her business, MSNW.

After spending several years working in management in another field, Janelle wanted a career that would allow her to give back to her community and offered scheduling flexibility so she could spend time with her young children. It was that quest that landed her in the cleaning industry.

"As you talk with people in this industry, I've found that no one really makes cleaning their goal," she said with a laugh. "But once we fall into it, it's in our blood and we stay."

Similar to the startup stories of many technology company giants, Janelle started the business out of her home and operated it from there for many years while her children were young. She managed all aspects of the business from her home base, often holding team meetings, taking client calls and warehousing cleaning supplies. By maintaining her commitment to quality service as she promised during her very first team meeting, she steadily grew the business.

"We didn't do any advertising," she said. "Our small team just took great care of our clients and we grew with them. It created some very strong partner relationships."

As their clients' businesses grew, MSNW grew with them, both geographically and in the scope of services they offered. MSNW evolved from a strictly janitorial service operation serving Whatcom County to a full-scale facility services company serving most of the Pacific Northwest. As clients requested new services, such as landscaping or snow removal, Janelle added those specialists to her team as they made sense for the business.

Today, MSNW is an extremely successful facility management business with approximately 400 employees, and several subcontracting partners. It was named as one of the fastest growing companies by Inc. Magazine and Puget Sound Business Journal. Their slogan "We'll take care of it," guides their operation and drives everything they do from their company culture, client services and community involvement.

Janelle says a key to her success was her ability to "take off hats" and hire the right people who could assume responsibilities within the business as it grew. She sees this as an area where some business leaders falter and unintentionally stunt their growth opportunity.

"It's important to have a business plan where you are clear on your own strengths," she advised. "You need be able to delegate and to take off those hats. Surrounding yourself with great people who share your values is paramount. I have an amazing team of people at MSNW who care for the business and our facilities as if they were their own."

A NETWORK OF SUPPORT IN CHALLENGING TIMES

Like so many in the world, Janelle was affected both personally and professionally by the recession of 2008. MSNW's construction business dropped 30 percent almost immediately and when Janelle looked beyond the business, she saw clients, community members and employees who were struggling.

"It was one of those times the world changed — it shakes you up and makes you look at it a little differently," she said. "There was so much fear and you could see it being a paralyzing moment for a lot of people."

She used the period as an opportunity to reassess the business. Where others may have waited until business stabilized and the outcome of the recession was clearer, Janelle decided to act. After consulting with close personal friends and advisors, she made the bold move to purchase the land and facility where their brand-new headquarters would be born. The new space would enable them to double their current capacity.

"You must pivot when those things happen," she said of the recession. "As a leader, you can't let those challenging times paralyze you and prevent you from making good decisions for your business."

She says without hesitation that it was the right move at the right time for MSNW. It positioned the company to take on a large contract the following year that it wouldn't have been set up for otherwise.

A strong network of peers, both within the industry and throughout various areas of business, helped her make that decision. She turns to this group at other times to discuss business challenges. Through her active participation in organizations such as Building Services Contractors Association International (BSCAI), she's made several connections which give her a sounding board whenever an issue arises.

"It is wonderful to pick up the phone at any time and call someone across the country and be able to share best practices," she said. "So often, one of you has gone through a particular problem before and can offer advice."

A member of BSCAI for more than 15 years, she became more involved with the organization as she realized the value her participation brought to her business. She worked her way up through the leadership to president of the international association in 2016, and will complete her five-year long officer term in 2018.

"I've done a fair amount of writing and speaking through the association," she said. "Now that I've grown my business, it's been rewarding to be able to give back and mentor other business owners just starting out that want to grow their businesses."

PRIORITIZING FAMILY, BUSINESS AND COMMUNITY

As a single mother for many years, Janelle worked to create space for her primary priorities in life: her family, her business and her local community. When it comes to managing the responsibilities associated with each of these priorities, she doesn't see it so much as striking a balance, but aligning her time with her values.

"I do a regular check with myself to make sure I'm dedicating time to each of these areas," she said. "Your core values are your north star that you can always come back to. They help you make good decisions for your business and personally."

She recognizes there are times when one area may require more of her time and energy, such as launching a new service at work. She likens it to an airplane takeoff.

"Just think about the amount of energy it takes to get an airplane off the ground," she said. "There will be times when all engines are fired and you're working overtime to get something started. But once that plane takes off and levels off in the air, it gives you time to step back and take a break and work on another area of your life."

More recently, Janelle has been able to combine two of her worlds, as her oldest daughter has joined the business. While her three daughters literally grew up in the business because so much of it took place in their home, Terell, the oldest of the three girls, started cleaning as soon as she turned 16 and worked other various jobs in the business during school breaks and summer vacations. Once she graduated from college with a sales and marketing degree, she joined MSNW.

Terell, Director of Business Development, has led the business through a recent rebranding effort and is continually identifying ways to market MSNW in new and innovative ways. Her two other daughters are still in school. Payton works in Human Resources at MSNW while pursuing her graduate degree in Psychology, and Paige starts her college education in the fall with a concentration in business studies.

GIVING BACK

Janelle says that if you've been blessed, it's your responsibility to bless others.

This commitment of giving back was instilled in her from a young age and is a big reason why she found a service-based company to be so appealing— it would give her a vehicle through which she could help others.

"I see it as a responsibility and a privilege to give back to the community," she said. "It's not just about business and making a profit, it's about community."

She works to engage her team in community programs which help them grow personally and as a team. MSNW has a "Care Committee" that meets and identifies different community-based activities that MSNW employees will participate in each quarter. This includes participating in Relay for Life along with other walks and runs, Cleaning for a Reason and organizing special drives for local organizations.

In addition to helping out members of the community, MSNW has a special fund, supported by donations from MSNW employees, dedicated to employees who fall upon hard times.

"We had someone who had a fire and lost everything," she said. "It was great to be able to use those funds to help someone within our family—not to give a handout, but to give a hand up."

To provide employees with the resources they need for personal growth and development, Janelle connects with other leaders to conduct "lunch and learn" events for employees on staff. The speakers at these events offer inspirational stories, education and best practices that are designed to motivate the team and help them.

Community involvement isn't just a company initiative, it's also personal for Janelle. She is involved in supporting several local non-profits, is a founding board member of Whatcom Business Alliance, an organization dedicated to fostering business and community prosperity. She has also served for several years on the governing board of PeaceHealth St. Joseph Medical Center.

Outside of philanthropic endeavors, Janelle maintains a commitment to building a strong community of business leaders. She authors a blog on management and leadership strategies, which she hopes brings value to readers, including people from within the industry and other colleagues she's met throughout her career.

"I'm very passionate about developing leaders both within my company and outside of it," she said. "If I can touch someone and offer them insights along their journey, I want to have that impact."

She has also started a leadership development company, Legacy Leader, with her husband, Graham, to help business leaders connect their passion with their purpose. In addition to speaking and offering one-on-one coaching opportunities, Janelle has created a CEO group that regularly meets to discuss best practices and strategies that will enable them to grow in their leadership.

MAKING CONTRIBUTIONS

One of Janelle's favorite business authors, Stephen Covey, once said, "Life is not about accumulation, it is about contribution."

In just a few decades working in the cleaning industry, Janelle Bruland has made significant contributions. While she's built a successful cleaning business in the process, she started with a commitment to service that is still very much a part of her

ethos today. Janelle continues to look for ways to pave the way for individuals within her company, people within the community, the cleaning industry and the professional business world where she operates.

As her company motto suggests, Janelle Bruland is "taking care of it."

Susan Chiodi

Name: Susan Chiodi
Title: Owner
Company: Helpful Hands Cleaning Service
Location: DeWitt, Michigan
Employees: 20

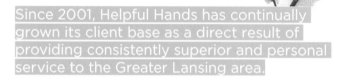

Since 2001, Helpful Hands has continually grown its client base as a direct result of providing consistently superior and personal service to the Greater Lansing area.

Where is home for you?
I was raised in Florida, but I currently live in DeWitt, Michigan, which is a small town just outside of Lansing. I plan to purchase another home in Florida soon as I miss Florida terribly.

Can you tell us about your educational background?
I did not attend college in the traditional sense, but when I decided to start a cleaning business, I attended an Extension Program from Michigan State University called EXCEL. I also spent many hours at the library and attended seminars through the Small Business Administration (SBA). I also became a member of the Association of Residential Cleaning Services International (ARCSI). All of these things helped me tremendously.

How did you get started in the cleaning industry?
I was a single mom working several part-time jobs, barely making ends meet. One of my jobs was as a caterer, and

I catered regular functions in the homes of faculty and staff members at Michigan State University (MSU). One of my catering clients got to know me and recognized my work ethic. She asked if I would be interested in cleaning her home.

It grew from there. I was so happy when I had enough home cleaning clients that I could quit the other jobs. I liked that I could make my own schedule and if I needed to take time off I could. This work has provided me with more freedom than I have had in years.

Can you tell us a little more about Helpful Hands Cleaning Services?
I am the owner of a single member LLC. When I started out, I did everything from cleaning to creating policies and procedures, payroll and handling human resource issues. After seven years of doing everything on my own, I hired office staff to help. They now run all of the day-to-day

operations. My responsibilities now consist of goal setting, finding new ways to motivate our cleaners and double checking financial operations of the company. I employ approximately 25 people.

What are some of the services your company provides?
We have decided to stick with the thing we know and do best—basic housecleaning. We tried some other areas such as office cleaning, window cleaning and allergen control. We decided that residential cleaning is the best fit for us, so we solely focus on that.

What do you like about your business?
I like the freedom I have. When you have good people you can trust in the office, it's an awesome feeling to be able to travel and not have to worry if the building will still be standing when you get back.

Have you had any big moments or breakthroughs that have changed either yourself or your business?
A defining moment in my business happened three years ago. I came across an opportunity to take on a very large client, Dart Container Corporation, which is the world's largest manufacturer of foam cups and containers. Their headquarters are located in nearby Mason, and they house their traveling staff in apartments for months and sometimes years at a time. My business now provides cleaning services in those apartments.

I was nervous to submit a proposal because if we got it, it would mean a huge spike in growth all at once and it was scary. Finding and training good people was the hardest part, but we

managed and it has turned out to be a wonderful business relationship. I am so glad I sent that proposal!

You've done an incredible job growing your business; have you had any role models or mentors in that process?
I would say the most influential person who helped me believe I could do this would be my husband. He is also a successful business owner and gave me a lot of practical advice. I also have been influenced by Steven Covey and his book The Seven Habits of Highly Successful People.

How do you stay motivated? How do you motivate your team?
Freedom motivates me. My staff, they are all motivated differently but one motivation that everyone seems to have in common is recognition and rewards. And they don't have to be big rewards—

we have a program where our staff can earn reward points and trade them in for a big variety of gift cards of their choosing.

Do you think it's tough for women in the cleaning business?
As a woman, I think I care too much sometimes. I come off too soft and too nice because I know what it's like to work my tail off and earn a low wage. Our operations manager is a male and he gets so much more respect and compliance that I ever did. Another challenge for me was hiring and working with my children. It's not easy to work with family, no matter how hard you try to treat everyone exactly the same they are still my kids and my expectations were way higher than they were for anyone else.

Nathalie Doobin

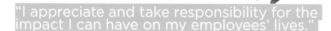

Name: Nathalie Doobin
Company: Harvard Services Group, Inc.
Position: Owner & CEO

> "I appreciate and take responsibility for the impact I can have on my employees' lives."

Was there any specific catalyst that first made you entertain becoming an entrepreneur?
Before becoming an entrepreneur, I spent my career leading teams, building brands and driving innovation globally for Fortune 500 companies. After spending 17 wonderful years in the corporate world, I was ready for a new challenge which coincided with the opportunity to own my own business in the janitorial industry—an industry in which my husband's family had been active in since 1961.

When did you first realize it might be a great career option for you?
I had the opportunity to attend a global industry conference, the World Federation of Building Service Contractors (WFBSC), in New Zealand. There, I was able to meet several industry leaders from some of the largest janitorial companies in the world such as OCS Group's former CEO, Chris Cracknell. I also met Sally Schopmeyer, president of Maintenance, Inc., who was the president of The Building Services Contractors Association International (BSCAI) at the time.

One of the things that stood out to me was the longevity of the leaders in the industry— Chris was with OCS for more than 38 years and was CEO for 19 of them, while Sally was with her company for more than 20 years.

What were some of the primary considerations that influenced your decision to become an entrepreneur?
As they say, timing is everything! Having worked for several pharmaceutical companies, I was lucky enough to have survived multiple company mergers. When I was presented with the opportunity to own my business in the janitorial industry, I soon understood that I could thrive on my own and become a valuable strategic business partner to many of the larger organizations by getting my company certified as "women-owned" by Women's Business Enterprise National Council (WBENC). Today, my company is considered a large company in the industry, and I am able to provide work to thousands of people.

When you need to make a big decision, how do you go about it?
I like to know the facts and options to reduce risk when possible. As such, I consult subject matter experts whenever possible and seek my team's input. Typical questions I ask before making a big decision include: Is this good/safe for the people who do the work? Will this impact the client in a positive manner? Will this make the company better long term?

Did you receive any advice that influenced your decision to become a business owner?
While attending industry conferences for BSCAI and WFBSC, I had the pleasure of getting to know industry leaders and leading janitorial business owners around the world for a few years prior to owning my own maintenance company. I saw firsthand the impact they had on their employees' lives, and wanted the opportunity to do so as well.

What are some of the primary differences you've found between working in the corporate world and being the Owner and CEO of a family business?
The family aspect of the business is compelling to me, especially the ability to directly impact culture. The sense of commitment and ownership allows for a long-term focus on employees, customers, suppliers and the greater community.

Do you have any tips for other women who struggle with maintaining a balance between family/personal and career?
I don't believe I have ever achieved 'balance' as professional goals and personal priorities have taken precedence at different times in my life. Recognizing that will help you find solutions for your unique situation. My advice would be not to wait for company-wide programs for an accommodation that can make a difference in your life, but to help provide solutions and innovative ways to address your situation, so you can continue your professional development and thrive.

Has entrepreneurship resulted in anything you didn't expect?
The "Global Entrepreneurship Monitor Report" by Babson College and other universities, underlines something that was quite interesting: Entrepreneurs are happier than other people. And in innovation-driven economies like the U.S., women entrepreneurs are even happier than their male counterparts.

What do you like the most about being an entrepreneur?
I appreciate and take responsibility for the impact I can have on my employees' lives.

What are your primary responsibilities as a business owner?
Ensuring the financial stability of the company to fund growth, and that employees have the resources necessary to safely focus on the client's needs.

How important is company culture to the overall success of your business?

The Harvard Family culture is extremely important to me as the benefits of a strong culture are numerous. Research shows that culture influences organizational performance, performance is defined in our organization in areas such as customer satisfaction, attendance, safety and productivity. At Harvard, we measure engagement quarterly, and have engaged with our business market leaders to help improve it as needed. Our inverted pyramid management philosophy has allowed us to serve our clients well since our frontline employees deliver service excellence at our client sites.

Any tips for managing email?

I have found that turning off your computer's sound and having your phone alert on silent or vibrate helps, so you don't hear the enticing "bing" of emails coming in. Having two computer screens is also helpful so you can work on one and have your email up on the other.

What's your favorite place to eat in Miami?

I'm a foodie who appreciates fried chicken as much as fine dining. If you are looking for a Spanish influence, Miami has a wide selection to choose from, however a Jean-Georges restaurant named "The Matador Room" is a favorite. If you like sushi, NAOE on Brickell Key is an experience. The best fried chicken I ever had was at Yardbird in Miami Beach and Joe's Stone Crab is a classic for seafood.

How do you relax and unwind? Any favorite albums, authors, and activities you'd like to share?

Travel is a passion of mine; I have have visited more than 75 countries and counting!

Is there anything not covered here that you'd like to share?

I'm humbled every day by the efforts our employees deploy to ensure they service our client's facilities safely and on budget. That's one of the numerous reasons why I'm proud of the Harvard Services Group Team and the many awards they received - JLL Supplier of Distinction, BSCAI Safety Award, INC 5000 fastest-growing private companies in America and Top 500 Diversity Business in the US.

In addition to being featured in Forbes Magazine's 2015 Most Powerful Women issue, I was recognized as "Enterprising Women of the Year" by Enterprising Women Magazine and "Top 25 Leading Women Entrepreneurs & Business Owners" by NJBIZ Journal.

I am proud to give back to the industry as an active Board Member for BSCAI, and as the Vice Chairman of The Hygieia Network, which advocates for women and helps combat illiteracy in her industry. I am a member of Young President Organization (YPO), Women's President Organization (WPO), BOMA and ISSA. I proudly contribute to my community through multiple organizations and charities, including Big Brothers-Big Sisters, WBENC, and the newly created Harvard Dream Manager Program.

Maureen

Ehrenberg

As the President of Global Integrated Facilities Management (IFM) for JLL, Maureen Ehrenberg is an internationally recognized expert in the facility management field. She offers strategies on leadership, team building, business planning and how technology is changing everything, from employee recruitment to the way buildings are cleaned.

Name:
Maureen Ehrenberg, FRICS, CRE

Title:
President, Global Integrated Facilities Management

Company:
JLL

Location:
Chicago, Illinois

Number of Global Employees:
+15,000

Education:
Ehrenberg earned a BSc Honours in Economics and Accountancy from The City University, University College, London, England. She is a Counselor of Real Estate (CRE), a Fellow of the Royal Institution of Chartered Surveyors (FRICS) and a member of Lambda Alpha International (LAI), the honorary society for land use economics. Ehrenberg is a Licensed Managing Broker in the State of Illinois.

Despite the fact that Maureen Ehrenberg leads a team of more than 15,000 people who manage more than 1 billion square feet of property globally, many people don't understand what she or her team does. In fact, she says the field of facility management just received its own occupation classification by the U.S. Department of Labor in the past year. At JLL, a financial and professional services firm specializing in commercial real estate services and investment management, the way facilities are managed, positioned and maintained is their core focus. Therefore, as the President, Global IFM, Maureen is constantly looking for ways JLL can improve, innovate and drive business productivity through the services they offer their clients.

Maureen's field has long been dominated by men, which she attributes to the fact that people who end up in the industry have often come by way of an engineering or architectural background. She's working hard to break that mold and pave the way not only for women to engage in the industry, but people from all different backgrounds.

How did you get started in the industry?
I've always been in the field of commercial real estate, but I started on the investor side. My background is in finance, leasing and asset management, everything from the acquisition to repositioning and maintaining of assets to the disposition. Basically, it's creating and enhancing the value for and of an asset or portfolio of assets.

Several years ago, I saw indicators that the facilities profession was starting to mature and advance into strategic facility management. Facility management, even though it's been around a long time, was only starting to be considered a true profession around the 1980s. This was an important advancement for the occupier side of commercial real estate, and I believed my background as an expert in investment real estate could benefit corporate and institutional occupiers.

Having now worked in both areas for a long time, over the last eight years or so, I've been more focused on integrated facility management (IFM) as it has been radically redefining itself and the workplace. IFM

has become an extremely sophisticated and integral part of the business to which it delivers service. What's happened is the workplace and employee productivity and effectiveness have become so important to the company—whether it's a production or manufacturing facility, an office building or a technology company, it really doesn't matter. The idea that place, and the productivity of that place, matters to that company is what's extremely interesting and presents a fantastic opportunity to differentiate and create an advantage to that business to recruit, retain and provide a place where employees can do their best work, every day. That is where we in the facility management industry add a tremendous amount of value to a business and to its brand.

How much of what you do concerns how the buildings are cleaned and maintained?
We deliver all the services to a facility—everything from setting the technology strategy and implementation of a smart building, smart workplace and smart experience to gathering, analyzing and reporting the data and managing all the services provided within the property, facility and across the portfolio. This entails everything from working with the business to define the desired employee experience to the planning and execution of the facilities business plan—the financial reporting,

benchmarking, lighting systems, heating and cooling, engineering, building systems, energy management, internal moves, to other services, such as reception, conference room setup, catering/food service and janitorial.

So, of course, in janitorial, we're cleaning the space and making sure it's kept clean throughout the day so that our facilities are always pristine, comfortable and safe. We talk a lot about the employee experience and human experience, so we want our teams and staff to engage with a high-touch, customer-focused approach to cleaning and comfort. This means great customer training for interaction in the facility and performance-based outcomes.

If you think about facilities management in general, when you consider the maintenance and technology approach, services were typically routine—everything was scheduled and then cleaned, whether or not it needed cleaning, via service level agreements within a prescriptive scope. We, instead, are focused on strategies that take a creative approach on how to clean buildings when they're not fully occupied or as space utilization throughout the day varies, as it typically does in a facility. Traffic patterns change each day. For example, if there's a company outing and no one is in the office that day, shouldn't the custodial workers that day or that evening do high dusting or address alternate cleaning needs outside of the defined scope that might not be so routine but will make a difference and yet not increase costs?

When you think about technology and sensors, if a restroom is experiencing high traffic volumes, we want to look at ways that direct cleaners to get into those areas more often during the day, and direct them away from the areas that may be on their listed routine but actually not in need of service due to low utilization. Alternatively, if traffic has been very low and no one has been there in the last four hours, don't send the porter there—redirect them somewhere else requiring service that we can pick up through use of sensor technology or badge card data, etc. It's a far more dynamic approach to the service delivery, which our customers are expecting across all of the services within IFM, not just in janitorial.

Which makes recruitment tough—how are you looking to change that?
I have been working a lot with the International Facility Management Association (IFMA) and the IFMA Foundation to create awareness for young people, especially young women, about the profession. We want them to know that there are many career opportunities out there in this field, in the U.S. and globally. We are working to create awareness of the FM profession at the high school and college levels as well as for recent college graduates. We seek to make FM a career of choice.

It's interesting, recently I heard about a study on Generation Z which suggested that this will be the first generation in a very long time that will not be college-bound in the traditional sense. The way this generation learns is through technology and the way they learn is very different, multi-tasking and learning as they need to. They are much more comfortable learning just in time and learning on-demand as they need to learn about a specific topic or matter. They're also much more comfortable with a non-traditional classroom experience. And, for example, they are open to online career training or an educational experience that may not be based on a traditional campus. They also look to avoid taking on a lot of college tuition debt.

That is so different than the thinking and desired experience of other generations and really breaks the mold for higher education, but I believe it potentially allows us to have more traction for this generation to look at FM. So, whether it's skipping college altogether or engaging in a trade school or apprenticeship where they learn about different career paths outside of the traditional ones, to taking an online education around FM and some of the core competencies—it could be a real way to not only create broader awareness for FM, but also develop more diversity and inclusion in the profession simply by getting the word out. If we can reach kids at the high school level we can introduce them to the FM profession

When you're reaching kids when they're out of college, they've often already decided on a career path. But, you have to be aware that a career exists before you decide if you want to pursue it or consider why you would want to do so.

What are some tools or skills you've acquired to succeed in your career that you'd recommend for other women looking to get ahead in a male-dominated industry?
Networking and supporting other women. I think it was Madeleine Albright who is credited with saying "there's a special place in hell for women who don't help each other." And I believe that actively working to help other women is actually very important. Sometimes within an industry, there can be unintentional biases but they exist and they are barriers to women or minority applicants who are looking to come into a field. Those networks that we can build and support are so important in making a difference for others.

We need to be supportive of creating opportunity and providing mentorship or actively sponsoring someone. We should also be tracking their success through the early stages as they're entering the field so we can make sure they are meeting people, getting opportunities to prove themselves and progressing. To just try and get established isn't often enough. We need the support of the network. I value very much the opportunities I've been given, but at the end of the day, you have to deliver, and deliver well. So, understanding what it is that you're responsible for, and ensuring that you're putting in that effort to get things done well is critical.

Today, the most important key to career success is really committing to it, becoming an expert and trying to achieve excellence in whatever you're doing. Industries today are so competitive, to just show up and go through the motions, it's not going to get you where you need to be.

What challenges have you faced in your career?

People can be reluctant—particularly in a field where women aren't in visible business leadership roles—to give women a senior role that has a tremendous amount of responsibility and a direct impact on the business and the profit and loss.

Many years ago, I was fortunate to be given the opportunity to become the president and CEO of a wholly-owned subsidiary of a publicly-traded company. What I needed was the opportunity and I was able to distinguish myself with the CEO and the board of directors, delivering the best team, business results, clients, growth and margin they had seen throughout the history of the company.

Ultimately, when you get into the position, you are responsible for delivering on the business plan, on the financials, gaining the respect and confidence of your leadership and board of directors. I'm very appreciative of someone having the confidence in me and making the non-traditional decision to give me that opportunity and executive leadership role.

What's has been the key to your success?

My team. Regardless of what you do on your own, being an inclusive, caring, transparent and motivating manager and surrounding yourself with people who are truly strong, hard-working, nice, ambitious

and collaborative will always be key to success.

Building a great team can be a challenge in itself—how do you do it?

The first step is to make sure you have alignment between what it is that your business is about, who are your customers, what are you hearing, what it is that you're delivering and what you should be delivering. Then you need to see if you have the right team in place to execute upon that. Maybe you have the right people, but some may be in the wrong positions. So, look at the way you're structured and see if your people are set up for success. Are they empowered? Do they respect each other and do they support each other? Leading consistently and by example is important, as the team has to know what is valued and what type of non-team like behaviors are not acceptable.

Work with that team; be a part of that team, making sure everyone understands their role and what they're empowered to do. Make sure they're motivated and supported, so we can be successful together and when we are not successful we do that together as team as well. We win together and we fail together. We address our failures quickly, we learn from them and we move on. That's important and the real key.

You also must create diversity and inclusion on your team. Make sure available positions are posted widely and through non-traditional outlets. You want different thought and difference in the way people approach situations. You want people who are motivated because they've been given an opportunity. It's amazing, what I've watched what people are capable of accomplishing when they understand you have their back, that you're 100 percent behind them in their success, and that success is everyone's success to celebrate as a team.

And then again, truly recognizing people's individual contributions through recognition events, promotions—that talent management process. It's one thing to administer staff, it's a whole other thing to have a strategic HR business partner that continually brings everyone back to training, career path planning—the last thing you want is to spend time and energy training people and have them leave. When people are engaged, respected, supported, challenged, rewarded, enjoy their team and what they do, they typically stay with the company as long as they can see their career path, progression and recognition and rewards.

Are there clearly defined career paths in facility management?
A career path in FM can be broad. There are so many different areas you could choose to go into. For example, you could come up through cleaning and decide you want a broader management role. Or if you're in engineering, you may want to go into smart buildings or energy management. You may want to pursue sustainability, become a LEED AP and start driving some of the sustainability initiatives that are so important to an organization and for corporate social responsibility.

There really are so many opportunities in FM, it's exciting.

What's the most common mistake you see women making in business?
The most common mistake we make is often seeking counsel from those we like and trust but whom often may not be the best advisors for us. Women constantly need to seek advice, because we are forging new territory. The feedback and counsel we receive is so important. Many women have a panel of people in place that they go to for advice and input on a situation, but we need to mix up that panel a little more. You can have trusted advisors on that panel, but consider asking people with a different perspective—people with opinions we might not like all of the time. Comfortable voices may not be the best way to go—your panel should be balanced, including those you respect but may not be that close to.

What's your source of inspiration?
I'm constantly trying to learn and learn what's new. One thing is for certain, we're in an era of constant transformation. And while technology is driving a lot of it, business is certainly changing. I love learning by listening and reading and constantly trying to understand what others are doing and thinking so I can bring a broader perspective to my clients and my team. The tsunami of change we are seeing challenges us to think differently about where things are heading. That keeps me very motivated.

Jamie Gutierrez

As a child, Jamie Gutierrez wanted to be an opera singer when she grew up. But now, she doesn't have any time for drama. Her straight-forward approach to management and the "radical honesty" she shares with her leadership team have fueled Midwest Maintenance's growth from a small, local contract cleaning company to a major player in the region.

Name:
Jamie Gutierrez

Title:
CEO

Company:
Midwest Maintenance

Location:
Omaha, Nebraska

A Favorite Movie Moment:
In "The Pursuit of Happyness" with Will Smith, he tells his son to "not let anyone stop you, not even me."

Advice to Other People:
Become comfortable with the discomfort.

Quotable Quote:
"Nothing that anyone else says about you has anything to do with you, it's simply their perception."

Nine months pregnant, Jamie Gutierrez approached the speaker after a panel discussion. She faced a critical decision that would not only determine the course of her professional career, but the future of Midwest Maintenance, an Omaha, Nebraska-based contract cleaning company.

"How do you do you it all?" she asked the speaker.

During the panel discussion, the woman, CEO of a large local marketing firm, had shared a snapshot into her life as the owner of a business, a wife and the mother of young children.

"I have a great assistant, and I delegate," the woman told her.

Up until that point, Jamie had always envisioned herself staying home to raise her children. But she also had professional ambitions—she had grown up in the family business and knew she had the talent to not only run it, but to lead it into a new era. Seeing that other women were able to successfully manage the responsibilities associated with work and motherhood was exactly what she needed to make her decision.

Jamie Gutierrez purchased Midwest Maintenance in 1997 and hasn't looked back since.

- - -

When she was young, Jamie's brother called her "The Latrine Queen." He shared the moniker often as the two helped clean the barracks at Offutt Air Force Base near Omaha, Nebraska, where they worked on the weekends. Her father, an Air Force veteran, had received an 8A contract to service the facilities and the kids helped out when they were given the opportunity. Jamie didn't realize it at the time, but the name marked her for life.

For many years, her parents, Paul and Alice Gutierrez, operated Midwest Maintenance out of their garage. The second of three children, Jamie cleaned during the weekends and on school breaks when she was younger. She graduated from high school with ambitions of becoming a doctor. But when she discovered she didn't like science, she went on to pursue pre-law courses that would enable her to become a lawyer and help Latino immigrants coming to the U.S.

One of the first in her large family to earn a bachelor's degree, Jamie decided her next move would be out to California with her sister. That's when her father asked Jamie to stay and help out with the operations while he looked to replace his general manager. Her sister moved to California. Jamie stayed.

"I always joke that I'm the George Bailey who stayed behind to run the credit union in 'It's a Wonderful Life'," she said, laughing. "But once I got in the business, I couldn't leave."

The company was still relatively small at the time, and Jamie worked various functions at Midwest Maintenance while taking classes toward her MBA at Creighton University. She became president of Midwest Maintenance in 1995. When her parents offered to sell the business to her two years later so they could retire and move to California, she bought it and became the CEO.

LEADING WITH AUTHENTICITY

Transparent, authentic, honest—these are three words Jamie regularly uses to describe the dynamic of her senior leadership team. It's a part of a transformational leadership approach that has enabled them to move quickly and helped drive the exponential growth the company has experienced over the past 10 years.

"If my zipper is down, I want you to care enough about me to tell me about it," she said frankly.

Early in her career, Jamie said she wasn't in a place where she could have that sort of relationship with her senior leadership team. In fact, she was scared to death of asking for feedback, because she was hard enough on herself already. But she realized that if she wanted to take the business to the next level, the culture and success of the company had to start with her. She needed to look in the mirror and be the change she wanted to see.

"Transformational leadership means that I'm showing up and doing whatever I can to make sure every single employee is successful," she said. "Similarly, I expect the person in accounting shows up so the person in purchasing is successful. We are all there for one another and we show up to give it our best."

As the company grew, Midwest Maintenance substantially pared down its senior leadership team rather than expand it. The team of four has since become extremely close, largely due to the fact they communicate with "radical honesty." Jamie said this allows them to offer straightforward observations and advice to one another without hard feelings.

"We move quickly because we're very transparent, open and honest with each other," she said. "We also have a lot of love for each other, which

makes it easier to be honest with one another."

The leadership has set aggressive growth goals, so they look to eliminate issues that could derail their focus. Concluding that there's too much opportunity for people to misinterpret what's being said through an electronic communication, they use e-mail and text messages primarily for informational exchanges. A subsequent policy requires all conversations take place either on the phone or in person.

Similarly, when disagreements arise about decisions that need to be made, team members get in front of each other and talk through it. Once they decide upon a solution, they back each other up to achieve the desired result.

"People tell me things I don't like and I tell them things they don't like," she said. "And it's not easy. I don't like to be confrontational. I like everyone to like me and to have fun. But I don't hold back anymore. And it's been amazing because now, when we get to the end of the conversation we tell one another how much we care for the other person and we move forward."

MANAGING BOUNDARIES

Setting clear boundaries is key to the way Jamie engages on both personal and professional levels. A self-described "control freak," she forced herself to let go when she made the decision to have children and buy the business. She worked closely with the children's father and her husband at the time to adjust schedules so she could work from home whenever he couldn't be there. This allowed them to watch their children at home, which was a priority for Jamie.

As her children grew and cell phones were introduced, the boundary between work and home life has become much blurrier. Jamie recognizes the need to unplug from work and tries to make this a priority, but mobile technology makes that difficult. Refusing to be tied down, her father never carried a pager. She realizes that's not a viable option with the way the business has grown. Instead, she has worked with her team to respect her time away from work so they know when to include her. It's a respect for personal time that goes both ways.

"It's not easy," she said. "I could work all the time; I love what I do. But the key is respect. If I'm out of the office or someone on my team is on vacation, don't call us."

Another area where Jamie has set boundaries is within her business interactions with males. As a female in a predominately male-dominated industry, she said that early on she also learned to set clear boundaries—or "be prudent"— in the way she conducts business. And while she feels that culture has shifted, she looks for ways to move in local business groups and tries to be extremely judicious when accepting lunch or dinner meetings with males. She does it out of respect to her husband and the way it might be perceived by someone else.

"I had a priest tell me the same thing—ultimately, you know who you are and what you stand for, but you also have the responsibility of a leader to portray the best possible image you can and eliminate the opportunity for assumptions to be made. Prudence is really important as a female leader."

COURAGE: THE KEY TO GROWTH

When asked about her strategies to grow the business, Jamie credits a mentor and coach, Dan Sullivan, founder of The Strategic Coach® program, for teaching her about The Four C's Formula®: Commitment, Courage, Capability and Confidence. Dan developed the formula following years of consulting entrepreneurs, finding it was a common pattern all businesses experienced before a breakthrough. Jamie has deployed it with great success.

"I'll never forget the first contract we had in Texas," she said. "We wanted to expand, but we were also really stressed—we'd spent a lot of money on the start-up and we weren't sure how things were going to go. We'd made a commitment, but it got to a point where we asked what we were doing—we weren't sure we could do it. But we had everything together, had the courage to see it through, and it went wonderfully. A week later, we were asking ourselves why we were ever worried. We gained a capability and the confidence to open in another new market."

THE FOUR C'S
BREAKTHROUGH PROCESS

Dan Sullivan, the founder of The Strategic Coach® Program, developed The Four C's Formula® following 40 years of coaching entrepreneurs worldwide. He found that every breakthrough success for a business typically follows the following pattern:

1. **Commitment**
   First you make the leap of faith, no matter how scary.

2. **Courage**
   Have the courage to see that commitment through and believe in yourself to achieve that commitment.

3. **Capability**
   Once you do it, you gain a new capability you may have not realized you had in yourself.

4. **Confidence**
   You gain confidence, which puts you on the path to an even bigger breakthrough. Then the process repeats itself.

When working with her teams, Jamie Gutierrez encourages them to take a piece a paper and write down a time when they did something they never thought they could do. Because if you've done it once, she says, you can do it again. You just have to make that commitment.

According to Jamie, once you have the courage to overcome the challenge and you do it, it becomes the new normal. It's just like life. She uses the metaphor of riding a bike: when you first start riding, you're terrified—you think you're going to fall or get hit by a car. As you ride more, you become more comfortable and you eventually start riding it without any second thought—it becomes your new normal.

In addition to the courage it takes to make a decision and see it through, Jamie feels it also takes courage to surround yourself with good people who can love and support you. She recalls a point when she was surrounded by people who didn't want to take on the contracts.

"There were years when people didn't think we could take on big contracts, but I did," she said. "Eventually, I got the courage to speak up more, and I got a team of people in place who saw the potential I did and from there, it just became super easy.'"

Finally, Jamie says that it also takes courage to dream big. She wishes that more people didn't limit themselves from dreaming big and suggests carefully watching the words you use when thinking about potential, because of how that can impact your psyche.

THE POWER OF YOUR
THOUGHTS AND WORDS

When it comes to thinking big and realizing your dreams,
Jamie says that the words you choose in everyday
conversation are more important than you think.

Listen to yourself speak and avoid negative language,
such as "I can't do this" or "I'd never be able to...".

"Your beliefs become your thoughts,

Your thoughts become your words,

Your words become your actions,

Your actions become your habits,

Your habits become your values,

Your values become your destiny."

-Mahatma Gandhi

"People say, I could never do that; or, I could never go there," she said. "I always tell my kids, watch your words because it's like as Gandhi says, 'your thoughts become your words and your words become your actions.' It takes courage to think big in the first place and think, 'I'm going to do this'."

JUST GO FOR IT

Jamie said that despite the fact that she's a female Mexican-American and doesn't fit the typical CEO mold, she hasn't let that stop her. She encourages others to identify what it is that they want, and not to let traditional barriers hold them back.

She also has found that leading with authenticity can yield great returns. When she is true to herself and her teams, she's able to eliminate drama and focus on driving great results—results that are the direct outcome of the big goals she sets.

"I'd tell anyone to dream big, have the courage to do it and just go for it," she advised. "I don't think about my competitors or people who don't agree with what I'm doing, that's only going to slow me down. Just stay focused on your goals and go for it."

Paige Horn

Paige Horn doesn't like the term "millennial" even though she qualifies as one. A former aspiring interior designer, Paige joined the family business, Dixie Paper, after her father was diagnosed with cancer. Now he's cancer-free and she's the CEO. Eager to take their regional distributorship into the next generation, Paige is identifying ways to keep their business competitive in a new e-commerce world.

Name:
Paige Horn

Title:
CEO

Company:
Dixie Paper

Location:
Tyler, Texas

No. of Employees:
91

Company Mission:
Dixie Paper's mission is to be the supplier of choice in the Paper, Packaging, Sanitary Maintenance Supplies, and Chemical distribution industries. We strive every day to earn the trust and confidence of our customers to supply the best products for their needs.

Where You Can Find Her When She's Having a Bad Day:
Stepping out of the office to enjoy the sunshine and a cold beer.

Advice for Other Women Who Want to Take the Next Step:
Relationships are so important, within the industry, locally— these businesses are so important so immerse yourself in them.

> There are a lot of women who are beating the drum not just for their respective businesses, but for the industry as a whole.

How did Dixie Paper get started?
Dixie Paper opened in 1976 in Minden, Louisiana, with my grandfather, grandmother, uncle and dad. It started with my grandfather's book of business from a previous job, and their lawn furniture, which was their office furniture. My grandmother was a bookkeeper by trade, my grandfather did the selling, my dad worked in their warehouse and my uncle handled deliveries.

In 1985, my grandfather had three guys approach him from another distributorship in Tyler, Texas. They were young, hungry reps with families and they weren't happy with their current employer. They wanted to work for my grandfather. From day one, the Tyler location has outpaced the Minden location by three times because of their book of business. Most of our operations happen in Tyler, but as things naturally progress, we'll move all of our operations here.

I've never heard of Tyler, Texas. What's it like?
Tyler is an idyllic small town about halfway between Dallas and Shreveport, Louisiana, with a population of about 100,000 people. It's a great time to be a part of the town, because they're revitalizing the downtown and microbreweries and coffee shops are popping up. There's a ton of oil money here but also a lot of philanthropy. So, a lot of arts and very little homelessness. It's a neat community.

You worked in the publishing industry after college—how did you get started in the family business?
After learning that my father had cancer, I wanted to be back closer to home and do something with the company. I moved to Dallas and sales was the easiest place for me to plug in. My grandfather, who is no longer alive, and my father, always believed that sales was the best place to start in the business.

I did sales for about a year and a half and I realized two things: first, that sales is not my gig at all. It gave me a greater appreciation for people who have that gift. Secondly, I realized that if we wanted to grow geographically, we'd have to improve our distribution system.

How did you learn the operations side of the business?
I was transitioned internally into marketing, but I never really did "marketing." It's like "roll your sleeves up" and whatever needs to get done, do it. So, I took on IT projects, led consolidation of SKUs and item description names, eventually switching our whole enterprise resource planning (ERP) software—random projects like that no one else had the time, interest, and sometimes skills to complete, so they were given to me. It ended up being great

because I learned every facet of the business by taking on projects like that.

Is it hard working with your dad?
My dad is wise beyond words, and we both have such different strengths. He's the sales and people guy, and I'm more strategically focused. He loves the tradition of the industry and getting out there and demoing products, where I like looking at numbers and thinking about e-commerce. We're a good team.

You wanted to be an artist as a child but talk about a passion for the analytical side of the business. Most people would see these as two very different strengths—can you explain more?
I think the tie-in is the experiential learning. I'll be honest, I hated my accounting classes in college, they were my least favorite and I didn't do well in them at all. It frustrated me to no end because there was no practical application. But now, I'm obsessed with metrics. I could sit there all day and look at financials; I'm constantly checking them on my phone. I loved art because I could get in there and get my hands dirty, so I think the common thread between the two is the practical, hands-on application.

As CEO, you're responsible for making the big decisions and setting the strategy for growth. What's in the works?
We're focusing heavily on e-commerce. Just by nature of where we operate, we're in more rural communities than metroplexes and big cities, so relationships are incredibly important.

In a town like this, our salespeople go to church with their customers and their kids go to school together. So him showing up at that account at 9:30 a.m. on Tuesday morning is still important. We want to use the web for a broader reach and as a tool for our sales people to focus on growing their business and enabling them to increase their efficiency.

How will e-commerce change the way you do business?
I think it will allow us to keep our fixed costs down so we don't have to have as many feet on the street, but quality feet on the street. The same number of sales reps over the years should be able to double or triple their business by using that tool to make their time more effective.

But that hands-on relationship is undeniable. I believe we'll never get away from that.

You're a young woman running an old business in a notoriously conservative part of the U.S. What is one of the biggest issues you've faced since becoming CEO?
I think the easier challenge, but an interesting observation, is that there have been times when I've not introduced myself with my title in a meeting with a group of men. It's interesting to see all the men shake hands first. And then their eyes typically gravitate to another male in the room thinking that they will be leading the meeting. Again, not a big deal but an observation. I've never run into a situation with a customer or in a board room where being a woman is an issue, however.

The biggest challenge for me has been with our tenured group of male employees. These guys worked for my grandfather, my father, and now me. And they're comfortable having the daughter in the business, but only if she in a marketing role or leading an IT project. They looked at my grandfather as a father figure and my father as an older brother, and now there's me. So any perceived change that I make is make is met with five times the defensiveness of something my grandfather or father would have done.

So, it's been very interesting leading a team of 60- to 75-year-old men.

How do you get their buy-in?
I think the key is knowing how to bring them along and let them know how much I regard and respect them, but ultimately holding them accountable for their performance.

It's all about those relationships. There have been times I set these guys apart and bring them into the inner circle of information so they feel more included. I want them to feel a part of the business, so I share a little more financial data and a little more insight on what's really happening. I ask them for advice and counsel, because they're wise. They've seen a lot both in the industry and in the local market.

There's a Bible verse: There's wisdom in a multitude of council.

Why is community involvement important to you?
For a long time, we had the reputation of being an "us too" type of business. And by that, I mean, if someone opened a business and needed toilet paper, they called Dixie. We were never really involved in the community.

Now, we're a business leader. You'll see our name all over the place. We support events, we're involved in the chamber of commerce and we're no longer just a business service. That's been noticed. We've been able to attract some great talent that way.

Do you have any other strategies for attracting a new generation of talent—people closer to your own age?
I think that our investments in e-commerce are a big differentiator for our business. Prospects see that we're planning for the future, unlike most of our competitors in the region.

But like most regional distributors in the industry, we're still trying to figure out how to transition from a culture of fully commissioned pay to what younger workers want, which is a base with a bonus package, etc. So identifying the traits that made those older and insanely driven, self-made sales people and translating that into different compensation plans has been a challenge.

What are some of the organizations you're involved in and why is that important to you?
I really think that in terms of finding a community and developing support,

particularly as a young woman in the industry, I've looked for organizations that partner me with mentors like Meredith Rueben and others like her. So, becoming involved with ISSA and the Hygieia Network, or Women in Network (WIN) that I'm the chair of. These groups have given me a non-competitive environment to get together with other women and talk about our challenges, both as a female in business and as the CEO of a distribution business. That really is helpful.

Can you talk more about women's influence in the industry?
Honestly, I think women are leading the industry, because they're driving change. It's been such a male-dominated space for so long, and a lot of people are steeped in old traditions and ways of doing things. Women are pushing more progressive initiatives and breathing life into an otherwise passé industry.

People have this perception that we're the lowly little toilet paper sales people, but that couldn't be more wrong. Cleaning does impact sick days, and it does have an impact on health. There are a lot of women who are beating the drum not just for their respective businesses, but for the industry as a whole. We're not just cleaning toilets, we're making a difference.

What do you do for fun at work?
We recently hosted our employee appreciation day, so we had a huge pizza lunch at every location and a big raffle. At the end of the day, we had an open tab at a local BBQ restaurant so everyone could come with their families and come play games, draw with chalk on the walls.

The air in the office is fun. We're always pranking each other and we have a good time. If you're out for a week on vacation, you can be darned sure something will have happened to your desk when you get back. I think that's a testament to our hiring, we don't just hire on a checklist, but we want to make sure that we're going to enjoy being next to that person from 8-5, 40 hours a week.

What do you do for fun personally?
Personally, I love traveling. I travel all the time. That really is my time to kind of check out, but when I check out, it's more getting out of the daily tedium. It's thinking about the same things but from a different context. It gives you a better perspective on things.

What can we expect to see from Paige Horn in the future?
I want to be a game-changer. I hope to take the challenges we face on a daily basis, and look for ways to develop programs and processes that others can model to make it easier for them. It's tough enough—in distribution, you're lucky to squeak out two to five percent in net profit—it's no joke. There's enough on a daily basis to worry about. It's hard to think strategically for the long-term so the industry doesn't pass you by, or Amazon doesn't swallow you up.

Dr. Leslye

Kornegay

Throughout her life, Dr. Leslye Kornegay has refused to be marginalized. She's successfully overcome discrimination in several forms, and now directs the university facilities management housekeeping, sanitation and recycling department (UEVS) at one of the top universities in the U.S. Knowing first-hand what it's like to feel stuck in a job, she works hard to create opportunities for the individuals she manages, making education and empowerment a priority everywhere she goes.

Name:
Leslye Kornegay, Ed.D.

Title:
Senior Director of
Environmental Services

Employer:
Duke University

Location:
Durham, NC

What She Does When She's
Not Working:
Leslye puts her health first and
works out whenever she can.

One of Her Proudest
Achievements:
Being accepted into the
HERS Institute, which is
an organization dedicated
to creating and sustaining
a community of women
leaders through leadership
development programs and
other strategies with a special
focus on gender equality within
the broader commitment
to achieving equality and
excellence in higher education.

When She Knew
She'd Arrived:
An employee returned from a
visit to his native country and
presented her with a statue of
a mother holding up her child.
She had encouraged him to
get his degree while working
at UVM and promoted him to a
management position. When he
presented her with the statue,
he told her that he felt like she
was the mother, holding up her
children, the custodial workers.

Recommended Reading:
**"Start with Why: How Great
Leaders Inspire Everyone to
Take Action"** by Simon Sinek

**"Race and Redemption in the
New South"** by Osha Grey
Davidson

After repeatedly being passed over for a front desk management position at a major hotel in Raleigh, NC, Dr. Leslye Kornegay became frustrated. She couldn't identify the issue: she had experience, worked hard and was extremely efficient. That's when another manager, a white male whom Leslye considered a good friend, pulled her aside.

"You're never going to be a manager, and I think you know why," he said.

"Because I'm a woman?" she asked.

"No, because you're black."

If she wanted to move up in her career, he suggested she try the housekeeping department.

"It was my first experience with workplace discrimination," she said.

"There weren't protections in place to deal with those things at that time. So, when I talked to human resources, nothing happened. It was swept under the rug."

FINDING A NEW WAY TO STAND

One of Leslye's inspirations, Oprah Winfrey, once said, "Challenges are gifts that force us to search for a new center of gravity. Don't fight them. Just find a new way to stand."

Leslye already had experience in the housekeeping department, so the dynamics and responsibilities weren't unfamiliar to her. Her first job in hospitality was as a housekeeper at the Playboy Hotel and Casino in Atlantic City. After returning to her home state of North Carolina, she returned to housekeeping once again—at the same hotel where she'd be turned down for the management role.

While she wasn't thrilled about the prospect of working in housekeeping, she set up a meeting with the executive housekeeper who was recognized locally for her expertise in the field. The woman saw Leslye's potential and took her under her wing, hiring her as the assistant director.

Leslye found that she enjoyed housekeeping—she loved working with people and solving the different challenges presented each day. She spent a few short years as the assistant before going on to open a new four-star hotel as the executive housekeeper. In this role, she managed more than 100 employees, which included housekeeping and laundry.

She was in her late 20s and worked closely with a white male general manager (GM) from California whom she considers to be the second

FIVE STEPS TO HIRING A MORE INCLUSIVE AND DIVERSE TEAM

In too many custodial operations, the leadership doesn't often reflect the frontline workers. In order to create a more diverse and inclusive team — whether you have 10 employees or 10,000 — Leslye Kornegay, Ed.D., recommends the following:

1. Make a commitment to diversity. In order for any diversity initiative to be effective, leaders need to be engaged.

2. When hiring, consider different vehicles for marketing the available positions so they will reach a more diverse audience, such as associations or peer institutions. Don't be afraid to go outside the local area or state to generate interest.

3. Require applicants provide insights into how they have promoted diversity or inclusiveness, so even if you can't find someone of a different race or gender, you will continue to promote a culture of inclusiveness.

4. Make sure that you have a diverse interview committee that offers multiple lenses to review and identify with the candidates.

5. Set measures for accountability and stay involved in the process. It's possible that through the review process, individuals on the hiring team may unconsciously identify barriers (e.g. lack of credentials or education) that could easily be overcome. Staying involved will help you ensure that good candidates are recognized.

major role model who helped her embrace the industry.

"At that time, most leaders managed with an authoritarian style," she said. This GM helped me understand that emotional intelligence can be an effective way to manage.

Leslye went on to open several other four-star hotels around Durham, NC, before transitioning out of hospitality into higher education. Working at several large institutions including the University of North Carolina and NC State

University, Leslye hit what she calls "the cement ceiling." Her recent career moves had been lateral while friends and colleagues were moving up in their careers.

Initially, she thought it was because she didn't have an educational degree. She held several industry-related designations, but had never completed college. She went on to complete her associate, bachelor's and master's degrees. Once she completed her master's degree and still wasn't able to advance, she realized the reason she wasn't receiving promotions wasn't something she could change.

"Inclusion, diversity, race, the fact that I'm a female—that always was the last factor I'd consider if I didn't get the job," she said. "I always assumed it was my lack of experience or education. I finally realized that wasn't what was blocking my progress."

Seeking a new center of gravity, Leslye once again found a new way to stand—in a different part of the country. In her early 40s, Leslye made a leap of faith and moved from North Carolina to New England. She accepted a position as an associate director at the University of Massachusetts. Here she was responsible for managing all campus housing facilities, which included maintenance, grounds, housekeeping and event planning. She completely reorganized the department, quickly finding it was something she was extremely skilled at doing.

The next big step in her career was to the University of Vermont (UVM) where she accepted a position as the Director of the Facilities Division, Department of Custodial Services. Here she assumed the daunting responsibility of completely reorganizing and centralizing all of the custodial operations for 5 million cleanable square feet into a single department. Her team included union and non-unionized workers representing 22 languages.

At the conclusion of the reorganization, she achieved a $3 million cost savings through service level changes, redesigning existing positions and empowering and promoting frontline staff.

"There were a number of things I put in place early on that enabled us to efficiently track our performance," she said. "As a result, if we ever had a budget reduction, we were able to make adjustments without laying off any of our employees."

CREATING OPPORTUNITIES FOR OTHERS

Because she's experienced the frustration of being "stuck" in her career, Leslye works hard to create opportunities for the individuals she manages through education and certification courses. At UVM, she dedicated a significant portion of her budget to training, requiring that all custodial managers and supervisors take a 360-hour industry education program together, three to four hours a week. Frontline employees were also required to participate in an annual departmental in-service.

"It wasn't just about getting them through that educational series," she said. "It was about building a team. Having gone through the certification program myself, I learned a lot, and I wanted to model that same experience for them."

She implemented a clear career track to move employees forward in their careers, from frontline employees through management. Advancement opportunities were based

FROM THE SEGREGATED SOUTH TO THE MULTICULTURAL MILITARY

Growing up, Leslye's father was in the Air Force, so her family moved throughout various bases within the U.S. and Japan. This taught her how to be flexible and learn to adapt quickly.

"Military schools were integrated before the public school system," she said. "I went to a segregated school for the first couple of years, before going to an integrated classroom where a lot of my friends were from all different races and ethnic backgrounds. There were also a lot of interracial families. That diversity exposed me to a lot at a very young age and helped me appreciate different perspectives."

She said the experiences during her childhood helped her understand the principles of "The Platinum Rule" which suggests people "treat others the way they want to be treated." It also helped inform her beliefs as a "womanist," a phrase coined by Alice Walker, author of "The Color Purple," which translates into "having or expressing a belief in or respect for women in their talents and abilities, beyond the boundaries of race and class."[1]

"I don't know that I would be in the same place today had I not done those things," she said.

on education and work experience. This helped keep staff members on track and excited about potential career opportunities. She suggests that if more cleaning managers and directors promoted from within and charted career paths for their employees, the industry wouldn't have such a difficult time with turnover.

"In this field, we use technology, and there's also a lot of written and verbal communication required so it requires a skilled employee," she said. "But often times, the wages don't line up with the experience we need. I've found that in order to get that kind of talent sometimes, you may need to grow it from within."

But her commitment to making opportunities available to others goes beyond her staff. She also wants to find ways to empower women and people of color. At UVM, she served on the President's Commission for Inclusive Excellence, which enabled her to align the strategic goals of her department with the goals of the University. This included using diverse suppliers whenever there was an opportunity.

"Diversity makes everything so much richer," she said. "And it doesn't necessarily mean people of different ethnic groups race or gender — just having people who offer differing perspectives makes things so much better. That way you don't box yourself in and limit your potential."

OPPORTUNITY CLOSER TO HOME

After spending more than a decade in the Northeast, Leslye returned to North Carolina to accept a position as the Senior Director of Environmental Services at Duke University. She's the first female director in the department's history to serve in this role. She leads a team of more than 290 employees across the facilities management, housekeeping, sanitation and recycling groups on Duke's main campus.

As she reflects on her career, she doesn't dwell on the adversity and discrimination she's overcome, but is more focused on how she persevered.

"Thinking back, it's not that I wanted to prove anyone wrong, I just wanted to be the best at what I did."

Her acceptance to the HERS Institute, an elite program dedicated to creating a community of women leaders in higher education, further affirmed that she had made the right choice by following a career in the cleaning industry.

"[Applying for entry is] an extremely rigorous process,

and most institutions only send two people each year," she said. "I didn't make it the first year. The next year I applied, budgets were cut and there was only one position available. I didn't think there was a chance I would be appointed. But I was."

She feels personal networks are essential for any woman who wants to achieve professional success and examined the concept in her dissertation, coining the phrase "confidence circles." She defines "networks" as "communities of individuals who have your best interest in mind and will offer honest, purposeful feedback and advice. And individuals with whom you would give the same." Participating in year-long HERS program helped her extend her network of female leaders, whom she can call on for support.

"At the HERS Institute, I was alongside women who would go on and become presidents, vice presidents, faculty leaders—there was a wide range of women," she said. "I have a lot to contribute and being accepted into this program validated that."

And Leslye does have a lot to contribute. The experiences and challenges of the past have not defined her; they have served as a catalyst for something bigger and better. And her journey is far from over. Oprah said, "I was raised to believe that excellence is the best deterrent to racism or sexism."

And when you look at Leslye Kornegay's resume, excellence is exactly what you'll see.

1 https://ahdictionary.com/word/search. html?q=womanism

Keanon Kyles

He says it's not a dramatic "Singing in the Rain" type of performance, but when Keanon Kyles cleans the restrooms at the television studio where he works, he looks in the mirror and acts out parts of an opera. A trained classical musician, Keanon never imagined his career path would lead him to become a janitor, but it's a job that offers him flexibility to pursue his dream of becoming a professional opera singer.

Name:
Keanon Kyles

Title:
Janitor

Location:
Chicago, Illinois

Favorite Food:
Tacos

What He Wants to Be When He Grows Up:
An Opera Singer

Where He Finds Inspiration:
His family and neighborhood surroundings

All-Time Favorite Musician:
Andrew Schultze

Keanon Kyles has three jobs: he performs, he coaches and he cleans. Cleaning is the only thing he does on a full-time basis, but it pays for his studio space and musical pursuits. It's not what he imaged he'd be doing at this point, but he's learned to enjoy it.

Keanon's first full-time cleaning job was third-shift at a major television studio in downtown Chicago. When the sidewalks were free of shoppers and tourists, Keanon walked slowly to work, past the brightly lit Chicago Theater. He looked up at the marquee and imagined what it would be like when he would finally see his name there.

As he entered the empty, nearby building where he worked, it was quiet, filled only with the sounds of cleaners on other floors and occasional noises from the newsroom. Despite wanting a career filled with sound, Keanon appreciated the quiet and solitude because it allowed him the opportunity to sing. Keanon is always singing, and during third shift, not many could hear him.

These days, Keanon works second shift which gives him a little more flexibility with his other jobs. When he's done cleaning for the evening, he often goes home to sleep before returning the next morning to coach a student in his studio, which is located not far from where he works. On some weekends, Keanon has recitals and performances at small theaters around the city.

It's been seven years since he started cleaning, and Keanon Kyles is confident his days of putting on his janitor's uniform are numbered as he prepares for his first lead role in an opera. But he says that his experiences cleaning buildings have given him vast insights into himself, the people around him and the stigma that is associated with janitorial work.

SINGING FROM THE START

Originally from the south side of Chicago, Keanon started singing at an early age. His mother encouraged him to pursue his musical passions, signing him up for the Chicago Children's Choir when he was seven years old. In the choir, he was exposed to music from all over the world, but it was classical music that grabbed him from the beginning.

"I don't know if it was because it was so eclectic, so different or so demanding," he said. "I really can't pinpoint one thing that pulls in so much because there are so many special variables in classical/opera music but I do know what has always remained was my love for it then and my love for it now."

Once Keanon graduated from high school, he went on to study vocal performance at Columbia College Chicago, a non-profit liberal arts college in Chicago that specializes in arts and media. He concentrated on classical voice performance.

Knowing that he wanted to pursue a career in music, Keanon looked for jobs after college that would offer versatility so he could supplement his career with coaching and musical performances. He started working as a part-time janitor and was rotated between buildings before he accepted a full-time position cleaning at night in the television studio.

The transition into cleaning, however, was difficult. It required Keanon to swallow his pride, because at that point, he had preconceived notions of what it was to be a janitor. He concluded that sometimes you need to make sacrifices in order to reach your goals. He also had to come to terms with the fact that just because people treated him differently because he was a janitor, it ultimately didn't change who he was.

"I had to silence a lot of negative thoughts in my head," he said. "I had just graduated from college and thought, why am I doing this? But I decided to make as much good out of it as I could. I thought to myself, if you want to work in the music industry and you have a job at a TV station, make something happen."

So he did.

OVERCOMING THE JANITOR STEREOTYPE

When he first started, Keanon realized just how hard custodial work is. He said it's not only physically tiring, particularly when you're juggling several other jobs as most janitors do, but it's also mentally taxing. It's people's thoughtlessness and disregard for janitor's work that he finds to be the most frustrating.

"Sometimes you wonder why people do this stuff," he said. "They know we come in to clean every day and they don't think to make sure that the tissue hits the trashcan and not the floor? What is that?"

He recalled another incident where someone spilled an open cup of coffee into a garbage can and it leaked everywhere. Someone from the news station later placed a note on the garbage can, requesting that people in the office not drop their open coffee in the trash. Not long after, someone else from the news station responded, commenting: "that's what the janitors are for."

But for Keanon, it's not just about people's thoughtlessness, but also the way they act toward custodial staff that can be equally as taxing. When he was transitioned to second shift, it was a big change because he had to interact more with people working late in the studios. Initially, he was reluctant to speak to them when he entered their offices to clean. He was afraid of how they would respond.

Over time, he's gained confidence when he comes to clean an occupied room. While he's formed several great relationships with people who have become friends and some of his biggest fans, there are others who have a preconceived notion of who he is based on his uniform.

"People just assume that because you're a janitor and wearing a uniform that you're uneducated and at the bottom of the totem pole," he said. "It's interesting, because their assumptions are so strong, they don't ever have to say anything. It's all in their body language."

When he sees people outside of work in his street clothes, he's heard remarks like "you clean up well." He's baffled by these comments, because they suggest that just because he's wearing a uniform that he's not clean or doesn't have any personal expression.

As he talks about people's perceptions of janitorial workers, he starts talking about all the other people he knows and how much those perceptions impact them. It's not as much about the way he's perceived anymore, but the way these perceptions impact other cleaners who have become his friends. People with skills and talents that may go undiscovered because they are oppressed by the stereotype and lack the self-confidence to overcome the perceptions of others. After seven years, it's not personal for Keanon any longer.

"I have a friend who doesn't speak a lot of English and it holds her back because she doesn't feel confident in her ability to freely speak when she enters someone's office," he said. "People at times just look at her and she feels awkward, so sometimes she asks me to help because she doesn't want to feel as if she is disturbing them nor does she want to risk being yelled at. When you feel like people think less of you, it's easy to get that thought stuck in your head. The next thing you know, you start to really feel like you're less of a person. She's an amazing worker and person, with wonderful gifts and talents herself that people will miss out on because they hold that perception."

GRATITUDE AND GOALS

In addition to providing a reliable income and a place for him to work through his performances, Keanon's experiences as a janitor have provided him with an opportunity for self-reflection and personal growth.

"At first, I was really upset about becoming a janitor, but now I'm so happy because it's allowed me to be grateful for so many things," he said. "It's helped me to really understand and have respect for all different types of people—from the lowest paid person to the highest-paid person in the building.

Another key thing he's appreciative of is the support he's received from his supervisors and other key figures throughout the studio. In the several years he's worked there, he's tried to quit more than once but he says that his manager won't let him until she knows he has something reliable to fall back on. She accommodates all his scheduling needs so he's able to attend performances or rehearsal. She wants his dreams to manifest in the biggest way.

"They have been ultra-flexible, whether I have a performance or rehearsal, they will let me do that and are more than welcoming when I return," he said. "When you're an entrepreneur, you don't often know the outcome, so it's been great to have the stability of this job while things play out."

He's also found support from the news team. Keanon lost his anonymity as the singing janitor when a producer at the TV studio talked with him and learned more about his story. One weekend, she asked what he was doing and he suggested she come to one of his recitals. To his surprise, she showed up.

Impressed with his performance, she shared his story with the feature reporter who covered it. His story has gone viral and has led to several opportunities for Keanon. He's soon to travel to Scotland, where he'll take on his first starring role in an opera. Keanon will be playing the role of Rigoletto in "Rigoletto," an opera in three acts by Giuseppe Verdi. He says he's excited about the opportunity and looks forward to what's in his future.

"Just a few weeks ago, I felt this reassurance that I wasn't going to be putting on my uniform much longer," he said. "I'm not sure. I believe I've paid my dues and I feel I've grown a lot since first starting as a janitor. I've gained what I needed to gain internally from this position. Now, I think it's now time for me to blossom."

Mary Miller

Refusing to accept the status quo, Mary Miller realized that the only way she would achieve her dreams was to silence her inner critic and embrace possibility. By challenging herself to pursue happiness, the then twice-divorced mother of three stepped out of her comfort zone. She has lived outside her comfort zone ever since, successfully building relationships and programs that have enabled thousands of others to identify and follow their own dreams.

Name:
Mary Miller

Title:
CEO

Company:
JANCOA Janitorial Services

Location:
Cincinnati, Ohio

No. of Employees:
600

About the Company:
JANCOA is a certified Women's Business Enterprise (WBE) that provides commercial cleaning services for Class "A" office space of 100,000 square feet or more. JANCOA also works with a large number of schools and medical buildings to provide a green and healthy environment for their facilities.

Where You Can Find Mary When She's Not Working:
Reading, golfing, at the lake with family or having dinner with friends

Favorite Inspirational Quote:
"Do the things that interest you and do them with all your heart. Don't be concerned about whether people are watching you or criticizing you." — Eleanor Roosevelt

At a time when Mary and her husband, Tony Miller, were looking to grow their Cincinnati-based contract cleaning business, JANCOA, Mary Miller said events within a single week delivered a one-two punch that knocked them backward and forced them to reevaluate everything.

The first punch came when Bob, a consultant hired to improve the company's procedures and margins, fired them after his first night on the job. Like many nights, JANCOA was short on staff and needed all hands on deck. Bob spent his first evening vacuuming. The next day when Bob came in for the debrief and planning meeting he announced "I can't help you. You have a people problem. Until you address that, you'll never be able to grow this business."

That weekend, Mary and Tony did a deep dive to figure out their "people problem." They purchased all the books they could find on hiring and keeping employees. They looked at what their key personnel had in common and why they often missed work. Their first big realization was that very few of their workers had access to reliable transportation.

Monday morning, Tony purchased a 15-passenger van, had it professionally painted and branded as the JANCOA Employee Shuttle and proudly drove it to the office to share

his solution to the problem. He also became the first shuttle driver, taking JANCOA's employees to and from work. While the effort solved the immediate issue of reducing absenteeism, it also gave Tony insight into the world of his employees—where they lived, the condition of their homes and how in many situations, several of them slept alongside each other in the same small apartment. He listened to their conversations, learning of money problems, children who lived in different countries and the other extended family members they supported. That flash of insight was the second punch.

When Tony shared these stories with Mary, their perspective shifted immediately—the cleaners at JANCOA weren't just employees, they were people with lives and struggles much like their own. At that point, the two vowed to drastically change the entire direction of their business.

"It's not about the task we do in life that makes it special— writing words, cleaning toilets, serving food," Mary said. "It's about the lives we touch and the ripple effect we can have when performing those tasks."

By focusing on the lives they can touch, Mary and Tony Miller have not only transformed JANCOA into a model of operations for other businesses in the cleaning industry, they have established a system that is resulting in paradigm shifts in businesses across the world.

- - -

"To help create positive change in others, you must first find the catalyst for positive change in yourself." - Mary Miller

Mary Miller understands first-hand what a grind life can become when you're managing the demands of children, work and a household. She was 17 and had just graduated from high school when she started her young family. As an entry-level clerk at a local shoe company, she helped her division expand their technical capabilities, steadily assuming more responsibilities over the next 10 years to become the operations manager for the Capezio shoe line.

"I'm a fact-finder. I love having data," she said. "When I learned those were strengths of mine, I was able to start feeding those more and came up in the business."

When the company moved its operation to Taiwan, Mary had little to fall back on. She had no college degree, three children and had just gone through her second divorce. Receiving little to no help from her former spouses, Mary focused on finding a career that would enable her to have more balance and enjoy a better quality of life with her children.

"Having a 9-to-5 salary job with no college degree was never going to give me what I wanted," she said. "I was more driven and hungrier than that. I wanted more."

She applied for a customer service position at a local mobile home dealership but ended up in sales. When the vice president of the company asked her to try sales, she laughed.

"He saw something in me that I didn't see in myself," she said. "I was totally taking the easy route at that point because I was being so stretched at home. But I decided to try it. What was the worst that could happen? It gave me flexibility and possibility. I could make my future happen the way I wanted."

Within the first few months, Mary became salesperson of the month. The acknowledgement fueled her fire to excel, but when she overheard a sales manager berating a male colleague for "losing to a girl" after a monthly meeting, it poured kerosene on her flame.

"The resistance fed me," she said. "And when people told me I couldn't do something, I had to show them otherwise."

She continued to excel in the sales role, and went on to become the company's business manager, handling financing and insurance sales. She supported three children on a 100 percent commission sales position.

A LEAP OF FAITH

Mary met Tony in 1989, and they married two years later, becoming a family of seven as Mary and her three kids joined Tony and his two children. Not

Even though she's the CEO, you can stillfind Mary cleaning office buildings if she needs to pitch in.

In a scene that could be out of the television show "Undercover Boss," she had the chance to interact with an employee who had been with the company for four years. As the two cleaned and emptied trash, the employee shared that it was because of JANCOA that she'd been able to get her own apartment, car and an associate's degree in dental hygiene. She told Mary she was in the process of getting a job and starting her career as a dental hygienist—something, she said, that wouldn't have been possible without JANCOA.

long after that her employer changed the lot hours to seven days a week, requiring Mary to work on Sundays. But Sunday was a family day, and Mary realized that if she worked weekends, she wouldn't be able to enjoy time with everyone. Even though she was on a fully commission-based salary and earning more than Tony, she needed to put her family first.

"It just wasn't going to work," she said flatly.

The alternative, however, required a giant leap of faith. A leap of faith, Mary says, that was like jumping from one cliff to the next and hoping to hold on by just a few blades of grass. A leap where there were no certainties, little support from her parents, but, as she would soon discover, unlimited opportunity. The alternative was joining Tony to lead JANCOA.

Tony had started JANCOA at the age of 19 after his father passed away. Looking for a way to support his mother and three siblings, he began cleaning bars around a local college campus while he was still in college. He took that knowledge and experience, left college, and founded JANCOA. Almost 20 years later, JANCOA had grown to approximately 65 part-time employees and was a small but sustainable contract cleaner. But Tony was ready to take it to the next level.

PUTTING PEOPLE FIRST

After Tony returned home from dropping off his employees that first night driving the shuttle, in the early hours of the morning, he shared the stories of what he saw with Mary as they lay in bed. It hit close to home.

"The more we talked, the more we realized that these are not just people to move a vacuum and a dust pan," she said. "They are human like us. They're trying to figure things out, just like us. I felt horrible. I had been so focused on my needs, that I didn't see their needs."

Mary describes it as an "Alice in the Looking Glass" moment. They had always looked for ways to help their customers and improve the value they could produce for them, why not look at it from their employees' perspective? What if they helped them overcome their obstacles, define their goals and help them improve their quality of life?

"Every opportunity I've had in my life started with an ugly mess and hairy obstacle that needed to be worked through," she said. "But having that destination in your mind, that purpose, that's what helps keep you going and gets you through those tough times."

Research has shown that most people who work in the cleaning industry view it as a transitional position, on their path to something greater. Tony and Mary wanted to develop a program that would help their employees make impactful changes in their lives and ultimately stay with the business for at least three to five years. It was then that the Dream Manager program was born, along with a host of other tools and opportunities JANCOA provides to improve the lives of their employees.

As a part of the Dream Manager program, new hires are given a form that asks them their dreams for the next three years. Then, the JANCOA "Dream Manager" stops to talk with employees during a shift, often bringing sodas or pizza. While the group enjoys the break, the Dream Manager talks to them and tries to learn more about what they want to accomplish, like buying a new home or earning their GED. The Dream Manager builds trust with the custodians and works with them to accomplish their goals. That might mean

pointing them toward a lending program that can help first-time home buyers purchase a new house, or organizing training and education programs for workers who want to earn their GEDs or learn English.

But it's not just about helping them achieve personal goals; JANCOA also helps workers realize professional goals that are outside of the cleaning industry. Ultimately, Mary and Tony realize that working against turnover is counterproductive. By embracing employees while they are with the company and helping them through whatever steps they need to take to get to that next goal in their lives, both the employees and the company can benefit.

The results have been staggering. By no longer viewing employees as a cog in the machine, but instead helping them foster and unleash their true potential, JANCOA has grown to become the largest independent building service contractor in the greater Cincinnati, Ohio, area with more than 600 employees and 40 percent market share. And even with 10 times more employees than when Mary joined the company, they enjoy a turnover rate that is 300 percent better than the national average. They don't have a single sales person on staff, so all their business comes through website searches, referrals or through JANCOA's community involvement. Fifty-seven percent of new hires come through referrals from existing employees.

"Life is like watching TV.
We each have our own remote control. While we can't control the thoughts that pop into our head, we can change the way we choose to look at each thought—whether it is positive or negative. If the thought is negative, we can choose to pick up the remote control and change the way we approach it. The choice is ours."

- from Changing Direction: 10 Choices that Impact Your Dreams by Mary Miller

In addition to its extraordinary impact on the JANCOA business, the program has become the focus of an internationally best-selling business book, "The Dream Manager," by Matthew Kelly. Through the book and accommodating TEDx Talk, The Dream Manager program has become an effective model for business leaders across the globe who are looking to reverse the trend of disengagement amongst their employees and provide the culture and systems to support their future dreams.

MARY MILLER, CEO

Where Tony is the "man behind the curtain," much like the Wizard of Oz, Mary plays the opposite role, eager to take the stage. In 2006, she became CEO of JANCOA, which allowed Tony to step back from the spotlight and focus on what he loves best—creating and innovating.

When Mary became CEO, it was a role that was unfamiliar to her, so she put her data- and knowledge-gathering skills to work. She attended numerous leadership programs through her local Chamber of Commerce and participated in coaching programs that enabled her to understand the skills she would need to lead JANCOA into its next chapter. These programs also helped her transition the company from Tony, as both her husband and the founder of the company.

"When Tony and I changed roles, I had to learn to have that dance and conversation with my husband," she said. "I wanted to show him the respect that he richly deserved as the creator and founder of this business so he knew that while we were in different roles, he still played a critical role even though I was becoming the 'face' of the business."

Through each new role she needs to learn, Mary said she gathers information by reading books, talking with others who may have insight on the subject and participating in group forums. But a key that she's found is just being open to potential and not limiting herself to the opportunities that could present themselves as she pursues a specific path.

The point that you let go, she said, is when true magic happens.

"It's easy to silence our inner coach and let our inner critic take over," she advised. "But I think that's important—fear can be a healthy component of our life, but it should not rule our life. I think that's what prevents people from moving forward."

MARY, CHASING HER DREAMS

In addition to her role as the CEO of JANCOA, Mary is also an international speaker, business coach and author. She travels the world speaking at conferences, to other entrepreneurs and to businesses looking to engage their teams and inspire the best in themselves. In September 2016, Mary published her first book, Changing Direction: Ten Choices That Impact Your Dreams, and is currently working on her second book. And where Mary and Tony had originally intended to sell JANCOA to fund their retirement, they are now working on their succession plan as several second-generation family members are now active in the business.

Mary realizes that she might not know exactly what is in store for her future, but she has the flexibility and courage to walk through the doors that open, and the ability to redirect the course if it's something that's not fulfilling her.

"We can write the script of our lives," she said. "We can change the way the results are if we're not happy and it's not feeding us. A lot of people have the sense that they're missing something, and it's easier to be comfortable in your misery than face the fear of trying something different when you don't know if it will work."

"But you have to have that blend of scary and exciting," she continued. "That's living life."

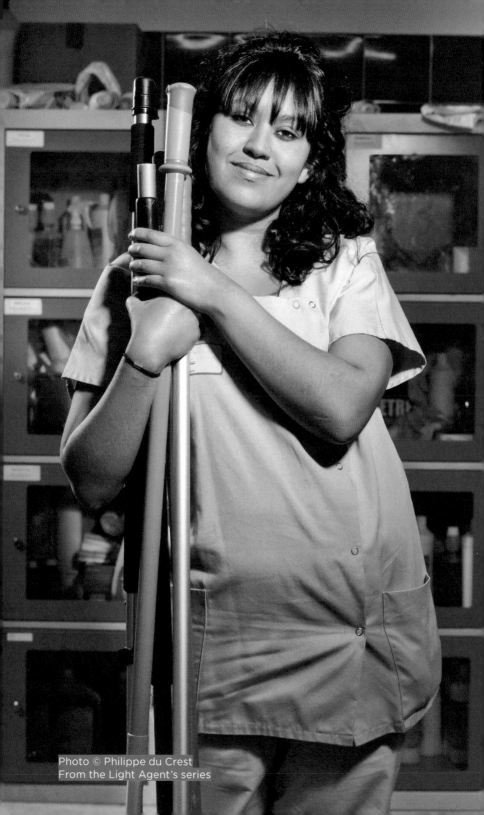

Larklyn Milstein

A native of the San Francisco Bay area, Larklyn Milstein grew up in the cleaning industry. During high school and college, she spent summers working as one of the only female window cleaners and as a station janitor before joining the family business, Lewis & Taylor. Now she's the vice president of Lewis & Taylor and president and owner of American Empire Building Services and hopes to help other women grow in their careers.

Name:
Larklyn Milstein

Title:
President, American Empire
Building Services
Vice president, Lewis & Taylor

Location:
San Francisco, Calif.

Her Favorite Places
in the Bay Area:
Stinson Beach, Ocean Beach,
Aptos Beach, Napa Valley and
Sonoma Valley

One Thing She Does Every
Morning:
You can find Larklyn drinking a
great cup of coffee, prioritizing
her day and feeding her vocal
cat.

Parenting Tip:
When spending time with your
children, no matter their age,
give them your full attention.

> "I work on employing as many good people as I can, supporting professional dreams, and yes, looking for opportunities to support the women around me."

As a child, you were a gymnast. Did that training have any impact on you today?
The main benefit from athletics is how they teach us to handle life and build resilience in ourselves. We learn to win but especially how to lose, re-focus our goals and get right back in the game.

In training and performances, you must react immediately to what's happening at each moment. I gained my sense of tenacity from falling down and making mistakes yet having to get right back up again and quickly!

Athletes know how to get their wits about them immediately when performing and we do it with real joy, passion, and total confidence—this is how I can roll with the punches in the business world every day. I really learned so much about adaptability and fast problem solving from my years as a gymnast.

What did you study in college?
In college, I studied adaptive physical education, which was the study of working with people who have disabilities.

Does that background have any impact on how you perceive custodial functions today and some of the risks involved?
Yes, absolutely. We're very safety conscious in our industry, so I get to use my knowledge in that area and am quite aware of what can happen. It also made me more aware of who we are placing within a specific environment and whether they'd be a good fit.

After school you went into sales. Can you tell us more about why you chose that route?
Working in bigger corporate environments enabled me to receive experience and training I would not have been able to get anywhere else. So, for my first 15 years after college, I learned how to negotiate and navigate the corporate world, working in sales for powerhouse organizations like Pitney Bowes, IBM and Sun Microsystems.

What is Lewis & Taylor and how did your father become involved with it?

Lewis & Taylor is one of San Francisco's oldest and most respected janitorial and building maintenance contractors. My father was attending the University of San Francisco when he first started in the sales department at Lewis & Taylor. He worked his way up through the business and purchased the company in the early 1970s.

When did you start working at Lewis & Taylor?
I started at a young age, working during summer breaks as a custodian and as one of the only female window washers. I learned the valuable lesson of how different jobs

fit different personalities and how the right combination can help make or break a successful account. I also learned to appreciate how tremendously difficult the jobs in our industry are.

Now you're the president of American Empire — can you tell us more about that business?
We purchased the business about five years ago, and I became the president and owner. It's a union service contractor. We provide sustainable green janitorial services and high-rise window cleaning, construction cleaning, power washing and floor care. We also provide cleaning services to office buildings, hotels, medical offices, biotech, schools, universities and the entertainment industry.

I'm also vice president at Lewis & Taylor alongside my father, who is president.

What's it like working with your father?
We have similar temperaments in our DNA. We're both patient and are what I call "stay-the-course kind of people," so it works out well. One of the benefits of working with family is that intrinsic common "language" you have with one another and so communication is smoother and more efficient.

What do you like best about what you do?
I personally get excited and proud when my customers are thrilled with our services and we land new accounts!

I thrive when I can help my employees advance in their careers. This is one of the big benefits of running these businesses. I work on employing as many good people as I can, supporting professional dreams, and yes, looking for opportunities to support the women around me.

I love working together with other industry leaders to help shape and drive both my own business and the industry to the next level—particularly as women executives.

Let's talk more about female representation in the cleaning industry—how would you like to see that evolve?
There are so few women in the industry and we need many more. I focus on working with others like myself in the business. We talk, brainstorm and work together to educate and help elevate our industry. This happens as we grow more present in the field and the boardroom.

Successfully working in a primarily male-driven industry, I've learned the delicate process of harnessing the best parts of the yin and yang of the female/male relationship, especially out in the field. It's proven to have huge results for my businesses.

What advice would you give to other women who are looking to advance their careers in the cleaning industry?
Join BSCAI/ISSA and attend their educational events. It gives you a place where you can reach out to other successful members, ask questions and seek advice. Join committees that resonate with you within these organizations and others in your community.

Work with your vendors, distributers and manufacturers. You can also join a peer group (a group of people who own the same type of business in other geographical areas of the country). This gives you a vehicle to talk about your business and ideas for how you can improve it.

I strongly believe in having the best team around me and bringing up those around me. I am constantly on the lookout for colleagues who I can help advance and grow—this is how I grow too. I often invite them to join me for educational or social events and introduce them to others in our industry. This is how I keep a fresh perspective on things, elevate my team and help other women make more contacts in the cleaning industry.

You seem like such a positive and upbeat person—how do you manage stress?
I'm a very joyful person in general; I do think it's a choice we can make.

I really don't have a regimented program or approach, but I do meditate, exercise and try to get out into nature as often as I can. So, if I've been inside either working on a proposal or running between meetings, I'll get out and go to the beach for a while or find a nice place to take a fresh-air break. I also think that having fun and eating well are keys to staying refreshed.

Can you tell us about one or two defining moments in your career?
The first was when I took on American Empire and became the president. The second was when I was elected to

the board of Building Service Contractors Association International (BSCAI). It's been great to participate in a peer group with other owners so we can share ideas and grow our businesses together.

You seem to spend a lot of time negotiating union contracts. Are you often the only woman in these environments?
The advantage of having women in these negotiations is it keeps the room "civil," if you will, and having us there changes the outcome to be more just—including a more well-rounded contract.

It sounds like an intense environment. Do you ever get intimidated when you're negotiating contracts?
I was the global systems integrated partner program manager at Sun Microsystems and I was working with huge corporations like Pricewater-houseCoopers (PwC) and it gave me such great experience. I know how to sit at a table in a boardroom meeting and I'm very comfortable. I'm so glad I got to have that experience. I don't get intimidated very easily.

You're a boss, but also a mother. Do you have any tips on managing both of these roles?
My theory isn't very popular, but I think that in the first few years when the kids are little, if you can work part-time, that's great, but if not, daycare is fine. But when the kids get older— in middle school and high school—you need to be a little more flexible and be present for all of their activities. They don't act like they need you, but they really do. They need

your attention and guidance navigating the challenges of middle and high school as they look toward their future.

Do your two daughters have plans to join the family business?
It's interesting—I don't know if they'll join this business, but my younger daughter is majoring in hospitality in college and has an internship in a hotel this summer. My older daughter is working as a property manager and pursuing her MBA this fall. That's what I do, I service hotels and commercial buildings. So, it will be very interesting to see what happens with that.

How do you keep your team empowered and energized about their work?
That's something I'm working on. I think positive company culture needs to be based on what motivates each person— what's important to them. For example, I'm changing one team member's compensation plan to keep them motivated. I moved another team member up from an office manager position to a supervisor in the field for construction clean-up. So, learning what motivates my team is so rewarding and they appreciate my interest in them as well. I try to move people around to help them learn new roles and do new things as often as possible—that's how we're all growing together.

We also give our team members tickets to ball games. And we celebrate everyone's birthday in the office with a cake.

Wait, everyone gets a cake for their birthday?
Yeah, we have lunch and a cake for everyone. I've purchased cakes for some of my employees who have never had a cake for their birthday before. It's really touching. They get really excited.

Are your turnover rates low?
Yes, very low because we're union. We have a great wage, they get amazing health benefits and pensions. A lot of our supervisors spend their whole career with us, because they genuinely like working with us.

We also try to do a lot of local training and bring in manufacturers to train our supervisors—keeping up to date helps everyone feel empowered to do their job properly. In that vein, we're launching a brand new accounting system and putting a lot of our assessment systems online, staying industry current with our process.

What keeps you energized and excited?
Recently, it's been doing three things that scare me every day, like making a "scary" call or starting a project I've been putting off. Or if something triggers me and I know what my reaction tends to be, I stop myself and play with it before reacting, approaching it from a different place.

I also recently joined a peer group. It's been incredible to have other people to talk to about the business. There are four of us in different geographical areas so we don't compete at all. We host phone calls once a month with agendas to discuss each of our businesses. It's beyond rewarding to have someone to really talk to about what's going on in your business. Even with the many day-to-day decisions I must constantly make, for instance, I was telling my group how I needed a piece of new equipment to clean floors in commercial kitchens, and was contemplating all the many options. I had a demo scheduled to see a popular machine. Everyone agreed that it wasn't the best product for my needs and would basically just sit around and collect dust. I listened to their candid warning and did not purchase it. I really value their input because I didn't have to waste my time or money. I ended up getting something else that's amazing and working well.

What's next for you?
I want to continue growing the business, in terms of increasing our profitability and coverage area. Our level of service is something that makes us stand out so I want to continue to focus on delivering excellent service to our customers and maintaining those very personal relationships with everyone.

Personally, I just want to continue learning as much as I can about the industry. I'm also always interested in mentoring other women and being more inclusive when I attend events so I can introduce people to each other and help women in the industry have better access to resources that will help them grow in their careers.

From the Light Agent's series

Shirley Perlinsky

As a child, Shirley Perlinsky's grandmother used to tell her, "we may be poor, but we are clean." An entrepreneur from a young age, Shirley built a successful market research company in Sao Paolo, Brazil, only to leave it all behind when her mother became sick. Overcoming challenge and adversity, Shirley started all over again in the U.S., her passion for cleaning transforming not only her life, but the lives of the many people she serves.

Name:
Shirley Perlinsky

Company:
S&G Residential and Office Cleaning

No. of Employees:
20-35

Location:
Manville, NJ

Defining Moment:
I had a breakthrough in my career when I participated in a mastermind group for a year and completed a book study on "Think and Grow Rich" by Napoleon Hill.

Advice for Others Looking to Grow in their Careers:
Continue your education!
I'd also suggest networking and joining industry organizations, such as the Association of Residential Cleaning Services International (ARCSI).

As she knelt over a clearly neglected toilet to clean it, Shirley Perlinsky winced. Coming from a culture where homes were cleaned from top-to-bottom daily and deep cleaned at least once a week, she couldn't believe people actually lived in such unpleasant conditions.

Shirley was disillusioned. She had dropped everything in Brazil to come to the U.S. to help her mother, who had left her home country years before to open a residential cleaning business in New Jersey. Her mother who was now ill, but who had once told her that she could never have a successful business until she learned how to clean in the U.S. Her mother who couldn't recall the names of her clients or their addresses, let alone the ins and outs of the business.

> "The business is nothing without the employees," she said. "You can do the marketing, make commercials and get new clients — all of that is easy. But it's nothing without good employees."

Shirley had left so much behind, like the successful market research business she'd built that employed more than 100 people. Her own home where she had her own full-time housekeeper. Her friends and her neighborhood—the place where she could speak and people understood her.

She was starting all over again to carry on her mother's legacy.

...

In Shirley Perlinsky's neighborhood in Sao Paulo, Brazil, her grandmother had a reputation for keeping the cleanest home on the block. Seven people lived in Shirley's one-room home and there was very little money for food, let alone a trip to the doctor. Cleaning was how her grandmother kept everyone healthy.

Her grandmother cooked her own soap, using a recipe that consisted of grease, pork fat, ammonia and water. She used the soap to clean everything from laundry to dishes and floors. But even though they had little money, Shirley remembers from the very early age of five that there was always money for Clorox to disinfect the bathroom. The small, unfinished outdoor bathroom that was a basic cement structure with patched roof. The bathroom they shared with another family.

On the weekends, her grandmother enlisted Shirley's help to clean the house. For her efforts, she was rewarded with a coconut ice pop. It was through those early experiences, Shirley said, that her passion for cleaning was born.

While her grandmother took extreme pride in the cleanliness of her home, her regimen was a customary practice throughout all of Sao Paulo that continues to this day. Once a week, you can see Paulistanas pulling everything outside of their home — their beds, upholstery and rugs — to "kill" the germs under the hot Brazilian sun.

Cleanliness goes beyond their homes too — everyone in Sao Paulo typically bathes twice a day. Shirley said it was this attention to cleanliness that helped her and her two younger brothers avoid any substantial illnesses beyond an occasional cold for most of their childhoods despite having a diet that consisted of mostly rice and beans.

Shirley's mother was often working, so it was her grandmother who provided the structure and discipline that enabled them to thrive in a tough neighborhood. Only a few short blocks from the slums of Sao Paolo, Shirley said it was dangerous, but her grandmother ran a strict home. With a military-like discipline, her grandmother demanded proper etiquette, good manners and rule-abiding at all times.

"She was like an army sergeant," said Shirley of her grandmother. "And while very poised, she was strict and very set in her rules. She helped keep us straight and made sure we followed curfews."

Shirley's mother picked up jobs where she could, often finding ways to make money by buying and selling things on the street, like clothes. Her entrepreneurial approach rubbed off on Shirley and her brothers. As a young child, Shirley set up a kids' store and a hair salon for kids in the neighborhood. She played "boss," directing her friends to perform specific duties (which, she said, they surprisingly did).

"From when I was little, I wanted to be like [my mom]," Shirley said. "I always wanted to create my own destiny and be responsible for my own income. I didn't want to be in a situation where people could hire and fire me as they pleased. I always wanted to have control."

Shirley's mother left for a year to fight in the Nicaraguan war when Shirley was only 13, and the kids put their entrepreneurial skills to work to survive. They baked bread and sold it to the neighbors so they had money for food.

As she grew older, school became Shirley's outlet and she poured all of her energy into learning as much as she could. Because her family had little money, her uniform, food and school supplies were subsidized by the government—without that, she wouldn't have been able to receive her education. Her teachers recognized her drive and interest, and pushed her to succeed.

"I had great teachers who are responsible for me being here today," Shirley said. "If I can do it, anyone can do it."

Once she finished high school, she started a market research company, inspired by someone who came to her home to conduct a survey after she'd opened an account at a nearby bank.

"He asked me the same questions we fill out online now," she said. "But I loved it and I asked him how much he got paid to do it. I knew it would be something I would enjoy."

To start the business, she rented a room in an office building and hired a small team who would go from door-to-door and conduct surveys. She went on to be the first in her family to graduate from college so she could learn more about the industry and continue growing the company.

It worked. Her business was hired by firms like Procter & Gamble, Johnson & Johnson and other multinational companies looking to expand in South America. Ten years later, she had 100 employees who conducted surveys by phone.

"It was a great business; we were doing very well," she said. "We made sure that all the employees had their own computers and used the latest phone technology."

And then in 2001, her mom had a heart attack and everything changed...seemingly overnight.

STARTING OVER IN THE U.S.

When Shirley's mother fell ill, she needed help and Shirley stepped up. She sold her business in Brazil, finding that one of her greatest life challenges lay ahead of her when she arrived New Jersey. She didn't speak any English and went from running a successful market research firm to cleaning toilets. Upon her arrival, she immediately started working, accompanied by her mother's two "girls" who helped show her the ropes. Her mother offered a small notebook with vague annotations, such as "the house with girl twins, Monday."

Around that time Shirley met her future husband, Gary. He recognized some of the challenges she faced while attempting to get the business up and running and offered to assist her in getting some basic things pulled together—like a list of her clients' names and addresses.

"He called these people and asked for their last names and addresses so we can make sure we knew where to go on Monday," she said, laughing. "You can imagine that was a really awkward conversation!"

Shirley pushed through her frustrations, determined to start a professional cleaning business. She enrolled in English classes and began gathering resources to build the business. A majority of her mother's previous clients had gone elsewhere because her mother had called to cancel so often due to her illness, so Shirley was basically starting from the beginning.

"I hated the disorganization," she said. "I hated the lack of structure. I hated everything— the clients were expecting us to clean the walls, and they weren't paying enough for that. So, I got a lawyer and put together a contract saying we were going to clean this for this much. That's when we lost almost every single one of her clients."

Steadfast in her resolve to build a successful business, Shirley and Gary invested their own money into the company, S&G Cleaning Services. They did whatever they had to do—built a company website, purchased vehicles, marketing collateral and advertising—to create a professional enterprise. Their efforts paid off—S&G Cleaning now employs approximately 20 cleaners and three people in the office who handle administrative and operational responsibilities.

A COMMITMENT TO HER EMPLOYEES AND THE COMMUNITY

It's been almost 16 years since Shirley moved to the U.S., and she now has a successful, well-established and recognized business in a thriving community and a supportive family. She said that once she turned 40, a few years ago, her attitude shifted and it was no longer about the money, but the people.

"My focus is on my employees now, period," Shirley said. "I don't have to be a multimillionaire, I already have a million times more than I had growing up, and that's enough for me."

To help her team grow and develop, Shirley brings in speakers to provide in-service on different various topics, such as health and wellness and personal finances. By putting its employees first, S&G Cleaning has one of the highest employee retention rates in the industry.

"The business is nothing without the employees," she said. "You can do the marketing, make commercials and get new clients — all of that is easy. But it's nothing without good employees."

In addition to improving the livelihood of its team, S&G Cleaning Service is also extremely involved with its local community. It gives back through programs like Habitat for Humanity, Cleaning for a Reason, and Cleaning for Heroes, the last being a non-profit organization that helps connect disabled and elderly veterans with cleaning services.

"I appreciate every day I'm in the U.S. because I feel so safe here," Shirley said. "In big cities like Sao Paulo and Rio, it's very dangerous and you can't trust the police. Here you feel safe because of the police and military."

Shirley said she feels best about the work they do when they are helping others who need it. For example, if there's an elderly person whose children live out of state, the children check in with Shirley and her team to make sure the home is clean and report on how their parent is doing. It's because of the services that S&G provides that allows that person to remain independent in their home that much longer.

A CLEANER FOR LIFE

Shirley Perlinsky is no longer working for coconut ice pops, but she's maintained her passion for cleaning. There was a period in her life when she hated it, but going through that experience helped her appreciate just how much people need cleaning and how much good she can do by operating a cleaning company. Now she's her own boss and cleaning on her own terms. Shirley and her firm have won many local and national accolades for their commitment to their clients, employees and their community.

"I started my career with the ambition to be a multimillionaire—as far as possible from the poverty I was born in," she said. "That was my drive for many years, but now I want to help as many people as I can. My customers, employees and my community. I will never retire, because I can do this for the rest of my life."

Marcella

Ramešová

Name: Marcella Ramešová AJ
Company: ISS
Position: Professional Cleaner
Location: Litvinov, Czech Republic

I would like society to better understand what this work is about. Everyone takes this work as a sure thing but it's tough work and not everyone can do it.

As a child, what did you want to be when you grew up?
I wanted to be a nurse.

What was the path that led you into the cleaning industry?
I had small children and I needed a job only for morning shifts.

In detail, tell me about your present job responsibilities and your title.
I am a cleaning worker at Unipetrol Litvinov, Refinery, with ISS I am 3 years, I am in charge of seven buildings where there are not only offices but also production facilities. I provide complete cleaning work including day service.

What do you like best about what you do?
I have the opportunity to communicate with people and that's what I like a lot. I try to do my job fairly and I like helping people and doing something extra, even if I don't have to.

Can you tell me about one or two defining moments in your career?
There is no such thing in my career – my everyday work is so diverse that I enjoy it all the time.

Who have been some of the primary influences on your professional development?
Probably the firefighter team, I have worked for many years in their workplaces. We work together every day and we have very friendly relations, almost like in the family.

What is your idea of professional success? Quality service?
For me, the professional success is that I have been awarded by ISS, that I have had the opportunity to meet lots of new people and I was warmly welcomed by all of them. It means to me that ISS value their employees. Quality services? That means to me mainly high-quality work and communication; we are here for the customer, not the other way around.

What motivates you? How do you motivate your staff?
Appreciation, compliment and knowing that ISS values people.

What specific challenges do you face as a woman in business? In the industry?
I work in a risk environment which is dangerous. There is laid a great emphasis on safety and protective tools, which isn't always easy and pleasant for a woman. Sometimes we have to wear fireproof clothes which are heavy and uncomfortable, but safety first.

Do you have stories that bring this to life for readers?
We laugh every day – these are small things or various or we do things "out of spite." For example when firemen hide my cleaning tools and I search and search for them... when I start joking that I will leave the mess there, they give me the cleaning tools back very quickly and with pleasure rather than cleaning the building themselves :)

How do you cope with the demands of your position?
When I have a lot of work to do, I really appreciate when I can talk about these problems with my colleagues. And also sense of humor is very helpful. We laugh and things are better.

What trends do you see in the cleaning industry?
I suppose that trend now is an environment protection. That means the cleaning industry uses more eco-friendly detergents. Also, customers demands are more ambitious and difficult. We have to know all procedures, detergents, types of surfaces, which type of detergent we should use for particular surface to not cause damage to a customer's property.

How would you like to see the presence/role of women in the industry evolve?
I would like their work to be valued properly. Also I would like society to better understand what this work is about. Everyone takes this work as a sure thing but it's tough work and not everyone can do it.

Do you feel it's important to elevate empower cleaning workers?
I think that we already have a quite big authority. We have access to customers areas; we have keys from rooms where personal things are. Customers trust us. Cleaning workers should have an option to improve procedures. I'm lucky because in my work, I can improve some things.

What advice would you give to other women who are looking to advance their careers in our industry?
A woman, who wants to work in cleaning industry, should be communicative, nice, conscientious and neat. A customer very quickly notices if someone doesn't like their work and doesn't work efficiently.

Do you have a quote, verse or mantra you look to for guidance during challenging times?
Not really, I take life as it is.

Anything else you'd like to add?
I would like to thank ISS for valuing me. I've felt very comfortable and I've felt that I'm a part of this company – everybody accepted me warmly.

Sister

Martha Ann Reich

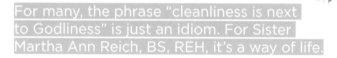

Name: Sister Martha Ann Reich
Title: Environmental Services Educator
Facility: Franciscan Health, Indianapolis, Indiana

For many, the phrase "cleanliness is next to Godliness" is just an idiom. For Sister Martha Ann Reich, BS, REH, it's a way of life.

How did you get started in the profession?
After first vows, I was assigned to housekeeping in the Sisters of St. Francis Perpetual Adoration Convent in Mishawaka, Indiana. During that period, I completed an educational program in the housekeeping industry through the National Executive Housekeepers Association (NEHA) along with three other sisters. Then I was assigned to East St. Louis to complete my housekeeping internship under Virginia Smart, CEH, who became one of my first mentors and taught me so much.

After your internship, you returned to the convent where you worked for several years at Our Lady of the Angels Infirmary in Mishawaka. Then you were assigned to St. Anthony Hospital in Terre Haute, Indiana. What was that transition like?
Within religious life, moving becomes automatic. You just do it. As a part of our lifestyle, we go where we are asked to go. I was assigned as a director of the environmental services department. A few years later, I began taking classes at Indiana State University (ISU). These were precursor classes for obtaining my degree, so I learned about microbiology and topics related to the cleaning field.

I moved from Terre Haute to Lafayette, Indiana, where I became a full-time student at Purdue University in Family and Consumer Sciences with an emphasis on Restaurants/ Hotels Institutional Management (RHI). RHI was the closest program I could find to a degree in housekeeping.

When you first started your career, almost 50 years ago, were there as many women holding leadership positions as there are now?
Yes, there were many women who were holding director-level positions. In the early days, housekeeping was always

94

a female-dominated field. Gradually, more men entered the field.

What are some things you did to move ahead in your career?
I served as treasurer of the Indiana Chapter of the International Executive Housekeepers Association. This experienced helped me to volunteer in other ways.

Do you have a specific scripture or quote you look to in difficult times?
St. Francis used to say, "Up to now, we have done nothing. Let us begin again." That's been very important—if I messed up today, I can always start anew tomorrow. We can trust in God and continue.

If you had to name three qualities of an effective leader, what would they be?
Be a person of integrity. And whatever you're doing, make sure you're doing it for the right reason. Have common sense, a sense of humor and compassion. Be responsible and help mentor others. That's more than three, but these are all important qualities.

Through religious life, you must have formed some close relationships with other women — both inside and outside the church. Could you talk more about why these relationships are important?
I try to see Christ within each person; it really doesn't matter if that person wears a suit, a dress or a t-shirt. This helps me to personalize that individual. He or she is made in the image of God, and that person wants the same respect and love that

I would want to have. There have been so many people who have been there for me to help me along my path and propel me forward. Good people are all around me.

I recently saw that your hospital was the first non-government hospital in the U.S. to achieve Cleaning Industry Management Standard Certification (CIMS), congratulations. Can you tell us a little more about that experience?
We learned about the program and Franciscan Health Indianapolis decided to do the CIMS program because it was the right thing to do and because it aligned with our Franciscan Values and Standards. It was such an accomplishment to see our team fully engaged in the process and finish the program. The staff was really pleased and grateful, because they were recognized for their hard work. I'm really glad we did it.

You live your life to serve God. How do you think the cleaning industry has allowed you to do that?
First, I must say how grateful I am to the men and women who have helped me throughout the many steps of my mission. There is no question that our profession requires a lot of stamina, knowledge and wisdom. It has been a wonderful experience helping others by encouraging others to go beyond what they thought they could do. As a leader, I believe in encouraging others to go beyond their scope and try something new.

Meredith

Reuben

Meredith Reuben left her job as a lawyer to lead the family business, EBP Supply Solutions, into its third generation of ownership. In her tenure, EBP Supply has grown from a local distributorship servicing a small area in Connecticut to a regional supply solutions business. Meredith reveals how natural curiosity, undeterred perseverance and focus can help you accomplish anything.

Name:
Meredith Reuben

Title:
CEO, EBP Supply Solutions

Location:
Milford, CT

About EBP Supply Solutions:
Established in 1918, EBP Supply Solutions is a leading distribution partner that provides a broad range of cleaning and foodservice supplies and services for businesses that rely on best-in-class insight, products & tools, and demand custom, transparent relationships. The company services organizations in the eastern United States across buildings, institutions (including government and education), healthcare, recreation, and food service markets. Headquartered in Milford, Connecticut, it operates out of three distribution centers

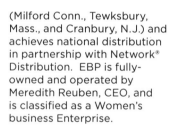

(Milford Conn., Tewksbury, Mass., and Cranbury, N.J.) and achieves national distribution in partnership with Network® Distribution. EBP is fully-owned and operated by Meredith Reuben, CEO, and is classified as a Women's business Enterprise.

On the Best Advice
She's Received:
"Understand the objectives and ignore all the noise." - Gerry Baum, her father.

Meredith on Learning:
If you're going to survive and thrive, you need to read, be curious, and constantly have a learning and open mentality. She surrounds herself with people who share this same quality. It's who she hires.

> "I learned to set an annual priority list. That really helped me allocate my time between career and family."

It was summer of 1979, and Meredith had just driven down from Boston to spend the weekend with her family at her parent's beach house in Connecticut. She walked in the cottage and found her normally jovial father seeming distant and melancholy.

"What's wrong, dad?" she asked.

"I'm trying to figure out the succession plan for the business and I don't know what I'm going to do," he said. So, the two sat down and discussed the options.

Most people who make their careers in the cleaning industry do so somewhat serendipitously. Not Meredith Reuben. She was in her late 20s when she walked away from her law career to join the family business, EBP Supply Solutions, which was known as Eastern Bag Paper at the time. For her, the decision just seemed right. But her father, Gerald (Gerry) Baum, couldn't understand why she'd give up her years of hard work and study at Tufts University, where she graduated with honors, and her law degree from Boston University School of Law.

"He knew I had run the gauntlet to get where I was in my career: I'd passed the bar and

completed several trials," she said. "Ultimately, I had a love for the family business and an inexplicable pull to join it."

The dynamics of the business weren't new to her; Meredith had been immersed in the business from an early age. Her parents discussed work at the dinner table and she regularly worked at the company during holidays and breaks from school. For Meredith, joining the business was a homecoming of sorts and helping lead the business into the next generation made perfect sense to her.

She vividly recalls her father's "aha!" moment—when he finally understood why she would make such a bold career change. The two were enjoying a night at the Lincoln Center in New York City when he turned to her and said, "I get it! Business is creative and law is boring!"

Meredith credits his openness in naming the oldest of his three daughters as his successor.

"It was fairly radical in 1979 to put the future of your business in the hands of your daughter," she said. "My father had tremendous courage to name me as his successor, and for that, I'm deeply grateful."

WOMEN DOT THE HISTORY
OF EBP SUPPLY

A quick glimpse into the legacy of her family business helps reveal why Meredith's pull to lead it was so strong.

In 1918, her grandparents, Samuel and Sadye Baum, started EBP Supply Solutions as Eastern Bag & Paper in Bridgeport, Connecticut. Her father, Gerald (Gerry) Baum, whom she describes as "larger than life," grew up in the business, working evenings and weekends throughout high school.

Gerry married Meredith's mother, Louise, while she was attending college at Wheaton College to become a physician. Fueled by a genuine love for Gerry and pressure from her own father, Louise gave up her career path to marry Gerry and focus on raising the couple's three daughters, of whom Meredith was the oldest. While Louise didn't work directly for the business until later in her life, she was always active on the sidelines of the business by entertaining customers and providing a sounding board for Gerry.

DEFYING RESISTANCE — IN HER OWN WAY

Gerry passed away just three short years after Meredith joined the company. Faced with the big decision of what to do next, Meredith talked with her mother, Louise, who had worked various positions in the company, including human resources leader. The two decided to keep the business in the family. Louise assumed the position of President. Their longtime Vice President, Jim Sugarman, stayed at the company in his existing role. Meredith assumed the position of Vice President of Purchasing. The team found that many in the industry doubted that the company could succeed under the leadership of women.

"We received a lot of pushback and pressure to sell," Meredith recalled. "And then the rumors started coming—people said that because I had a young child we would be selling the business."

In addition to Jim, EBP had a strong management team and they, along with Meredith and Louise, were undeterred. Supported by this team, EBP made an acquisition, which also helped put an end to the industry resistance and rumors. This acquisition strengthened their ability to service the entire state of Connecticut.

As Meredith worked to grow the business, she was also growing her family. She admits that it was a challenging time, as she balanced the demands of the business and needs of her young children and hard-working husband who was in law.

"As a mother, you are in operational mode when your kids are young," she said. "It can be stressful. But early on, I learned to set an annual priority list. That really helped me allocate my time between career and family. Sure, I felt the guilt, but I was there to drive them to school, and I made it a point to be home for dinner so I could hear about their day and do homework with them. Making that the priority and aligning the rest of my activities around that helped me tremendously."

While she credits having a supportive spouse, she also started a walking group with other women in the neighborhood. This sisterhood helped offer support as she worked to balance the challenges of career and motherhood.

"Women need other women," she said. "You need to be able to talk with others who understand. We walk in the early mornings on the weekends, so it doesn't interfere with work or family time. It is wonderful, loving support."

After her father's death, Meredith's mother identified a new location for their business operations. She and the EBP team led the move into a new 166,000-square-foot facility in Milford, Connecticut, just 12 miles north of Bridgeport. This enabled them to consolidate operations into a centralized warehouse. However, three years after the move into their new facility, Meredith and her sisters were dealt another blow when Louise passed away after a year-long battle with cancer.

Once her mother passed, Meredith became CEO of EBP Supply Solutions and Jim Sugarman was promoted to President. It was a new era for the company as Meredith represented the third generation of leadership in the family business.

Looking back, Meredith recognizes the many challenges she overcame during that period, including the difficulties of identifying how she wanted to approach her management and leadership style.

"Whether you're inheriting a company from your mother or father, or succeeding your position from a strong manager, one of the biggest challenges—particularly if it's going from male to female—is what kind of persona or style should you maintain?" she advised. "My father and mother had great names in the industry, and I quickly learned that I did not need to copy their styles or strengths. I needed to be congruent to my own personality and utilize my strengths, and surround myself with people who supplemented areas where I wasn't as strong. I needed to contribute all of my effort in my own unique way."

That effort proved to be ambitious—she led the company through several subsequent acquisitions and along with her team, grew EBP to be a regional distributor, which now services enterprises in all of New England and the Middle Atlantic states.

"MEREDITH LIKES TO HELP PEOPLE PUT ON THEIR COATS"

In her kindergarten report card, Meredith's teacher noted that she liked to help other children put on their coats. Her family regularly jokes about this, but she still carries a passion for helping other people and positioning them for success. This is evidenced by several programs offered at EBP, such as wellness, tuition reimbursement offers and mentorship arrangements.

This desire to help people grow and succeed has helped drive EBP's strategic plan. Recognizing that an organization can only be its best when driven by a diverse group of stakeholders with different voices and backgrounds, she is working with the leadership of EBP to set goals around diversity.

"I think it's easy not to establish goals around diversity when you're in a family business," she said, "Other priorities get in the way. We need to do better. It is critical—particularly in the cleaning industry."

Meredith works to empower women through mentorship programs within EBP, locally and internationally. She does this through local family business groups, the ISSA Hygieia Network and through "Women in Network" (WIN), which is a group within Network Distribution, an international buying and selling group. She wants to see more women in leadership positions throughout the cleaning industry.

"Being mindful of diversity doesn't necessarily mean having just one female or minority on your board of directors," she said. "They won't be that effective."

She details studies that show when you're the only person of your gender or race in the room, the group dynamic is completely different for you than when you're one of three or more. Being a part of a diverse group enables you to spend less time thinking and rethinking what you want to say. This enables you to express yourself more often and more cogently.

FILLING A MINUTE WITH 60 SECONDS OF RUN

As the CEO of EBP Supply Solutions, Meredith now spends a large percentage of her time planning the future of the company. She's surrounded herself with a highly capable team of professionals who bring skill sets to continuously improve the efficiency, productivity, culture and operations in place. Her son, Andrew Reuben, is currently the vice president of Marketing; Matthew Sugarman is the senior vice president of sales. The current president is Eric Peabody, who joined EBP seven years ago.

She says that succession planning is increasingly difficult considering how quickly technology and skill sets are changing the industry.

MEREDITH'S TOP FIVE
RECOMMENDED READING LIST

**The Seven Habits of
Highly Effective People**
- Stephen Covey

Good to Great
- Jim Collins

Islands of Profit in a Sea of Red Ink
- Jonathan Byrnes

The Mind of the Strategist
- Kenichi Ohmae

How Women Decide
- Therese Huston

While she acknowledges that she's in the final stage of her career, Meredith Reuben shows no sign of slowing down. She is an active volunteer throughout the community and industry trade organizations, an avid reader and very much still in the role of driving EBP's growth and development.

One of her favorite poems, which she keeps on her desk to inspire her daily, is "If," written by Rudyard Kipling to his son. The poem, equal parts inspirational and motivational, offers a set of benchmarks for living a full and successful life.

In the last stanza, Kipling outlines how one should approach the final stage of life:

**If you can fill the unforgiving minute
With sixty seconds' worth of distance run,
Yours is the Earth and everything that's in it,
And—which is more—you'll be a Man, my son!**

Or in Meredith Reuben's case, a very strong and successful woman.

Christine

Saldanha

Growing up in rural India, Christine Saldanha caught her first glimpse of the grandeur of the hospitality industry when she visited the Taj Mahal Hotel in Mumbai at age 14. After earning her diploma in hotel management, she realized her dream to work at the Taj Mahal Hotel which served as a springboard into a housekeeping career which has taken her to exotic locations throughout the Middle East.

Name:
Christine Saldanha

Location:
Dubai, UAE

Title:
Executive Housekeeper

Employer:
Crowne Plaza Hotel & Resorts

No. of Employees:
110

Awards and Recognition:
Recipient of the American Hotel & Lodging Educational Institute (AHLEI) 2016 Lamp of Knowledge Award for Outstanding Distance Learning Student, nominated in 2012 and 2016 for "Housekeeper of the Year" by Hotelier Middle East

Inspirational Quote: If the roots are deep, there is no reason to fear the wind. - African Proverb

Can you tell us about where you grew up and spent most of your childhood?
I was born in a small remote village in the state of Maharashtra in Western India. My family had limited financial means and our household lacked basic necessities such as electricity, running water or toilets. We were, however, closely knit and protective of each other.

As a child, I didn't have any exposure to the outside world and only imagined what it would be like when listening to my mother's stories. She had grown up in the city and her stories were a window to the big exciting world I wanted to be a part of.

> "The key to success lies in finding a balance and having a supportive ecosystem of family, friends and colleagues."

Did you have any dreams of what your role would be in that big exciting world?

As a child, I wanted to be a medical professional. I was always interested in all kinds of home remedies and traditional Indian medicines. Though I could not enroll for medical college due to limited means, I'm still an avid reader of books on traditional Indian medicines and Ayurveda.

Can you tell me a little about the career path that led you to housekeeping?

My father, who worked for the Taj Mahal Hotel in Mumbai, took us to visit the city during the summer break when I was 14 years old. During this visit, I had the opportunity to visit the iconic Taj Mahal Hotel. As a girl visiting a big city for the first time, I was awestruck looking at the grandeur and size of that magnificent hotel. I was so impressed looking at those immaculately dressed staff and way they conducted themselves. For me, it was an "Alice in Wonderland" moment.

It was an incredible experience and I remember telling my mother that I too wanted to work at the Taj Mahal Hotel. She said if I worked hard and stayed disciplined, I could achieve what I wanted. I eventually completed my Diploma in Hotel Management at 19 and joined the Taj Mahal Hotel.

That's an amazing story. What are you doing now?

Currently, I am working as Executive Housekeeper of Crowne Plaza Dubai. The property has 568 guest rooms with 13 food and beverage outlets and numerous banquet halls. I supervise approximately 110 employees.

My main responsibilities are to:
Keep the hotel clean and aesthetically beautiful, ensuring high environment standards and hygiene are met.

Participate in the preparation of annual departmental operating and financial plans.

Monitor budget and control expenses with focus on increasing productivity without compromising quality.

Maintain proper inventory levels to manage cost per room for guest supplies and labour.

Manage day-to-day staffing requirements, plan and assign work, establish performance and development goals of the team members. Provide training, mentoring, coaching, regular feedback and redirection to help the team manage conflict and performance.

Educate team members in compliance with brand standards, compliance with federal, state and local law and safety regulations. Ensure team members are properly trained and have the tools and equipment to carry out job duties.

Manage the quality of housekeeping laundry and spa services. Schedule routine inspections of all guest rooms and public areas to ensure furnishings, rooms, equipment, linens, public rest rooms, lobby, etc. are clean and in good repair to meet guest satisfaction.

Respond to guest feedback and ensure corrective action is taken to achieve complete guest satisfaction.

Maintain and order guest supplies and equipment in a timely and efficient manner while minimizing waste, and maintain "green" initiatives (environmentally friendly cleaning chemicals, recycle containers, etc.).

Serve as a manager on duty during the weekends.

Can you tell us more about the property?
Crowne Plaza is part of the Intercontinental Hotel Group, having more than 4500 hotels all over the world. This property is the landmark hotel in Dubai and is situated on the bustling and glittering Sheikh Zayed Road. It was one of the first five-star hotels to open 23 years ago. It is well known for its varied food and beverage outlets and famous for customer care. Approximately 35 percent of our clients are loyal repeat guests. There are 568 rooms and 560 employees from 39 nationalities. Our brand and superior service have allowed us to compete and thrive in a very highly competitive and fast-moving industry.

What do you like best about what you do?
Planning, organizing and executing departmental plans with my team is what I enjoy most. Using innovation and creativity to meet the daily challenges of the housekeeping department each day drives and motivates me. It's our ultimate goal to see the satisfied guests leaving the hotel after an enjoyable stay. Receiving guest compliments on social media and through guest comment cards gives me immense satisfaction and provides further encouragement to work harder.

I also really enjoy mentoring and coaching staff members. I have come across many individuals who have the ability to achieve a lot more, but who have been unable to reach their potential either due to circumstances or lack of adequate guidance. Mentoring such individuals and providing them with the necessary opportunities to achieve greater success in both their personal and professional life gives me immense satisfaction.

Can you tell me about one or two defining moments in your career?
Winning the "Housekeeper of the Year" National Award in 1994 at Mumbai India. The award gave me recognition as an exceptional housekeeping professional with the hospitality industry in India.

Another great moment was deciding to move to the Middle East in 2000 after a 22-year career in India. Moving to Dubai, where the workforce is multinational and multi-cultural, was a challenge and learning opportunity—one that I have thoroughly enjoyed.

Have you had any mentors or significant influences throughout your career?
When I started out as a housekeeping professional, there was not much available in terms of formal training. However, I was always determined to keep improving and learn from the best. I was a keen observer of people I admired and tried to follow their habits, work ethics and communication style, and build these into my work life.

I am especially grateful to four individuals who have mentored me and have been amongst my greatest supporters and a source of inspiration and guidance:

1.
Mrs. Elizabeth Kerkar, Vice President of Interior Design IHCL— She was a perfectionist and demanded high standards from herself and her team. She taught me the art of project planning and management. She always inspired me to be the best. Working with her was a truly enriching experience, as she taught me the importance of perfection and that nothing less than that was acceptable. Every time I met her or had the opportunity to work on any projects with her, I always emerged with more knowledge.

2.
Ms. Shirin Batliwala She was my General Manager at Taj Bengal and later served as the Vice President of Food & Beverage at Taj Mahal Hotel. She has been a huge influence on me and shaped my professional development, working style and management skills. She continues to be a mentor and friend to this day.

3.
Mr. Moussa El Hayek, CEO of Al Bustan Centre & Residence Dubai – He taught me the nuances of working in a multicultural and multinational workforce. His support and guidance in helping me understand and meet the expectations of guests with varied nationalities and sensitivities in a global tourist destination like Dubai was invaluable.

4.
Mr. George Farhat, General Manager at Crowne Plaza, Dubai. George has been a very supportive and inspirational leader. His support has played a big role in my success at Crowne Plaza. His unflinching drive for higher service standards, cost controls and meeting our owners' expectations pushes us all to do better and aim higher every single day.

From what I've read, quality service is a cornerstone of the way you approach your work. Can you talk a little bit about what quality service means to you?
It's often very hard to define what "quality" means, because the standards and expectations of quality itself have changed and evolved over time. However, though hard to define, one can always sense quality service. Quality service to me means to strive each day to meet or exceed our guests' expectations. It also means taking pride in leaving your own mark on the little things that the guest comes in

contact with, leaving them with a feeling of being cared for and looked after.

Housekeeping is extremely hard work with new challenges each day. How do you stay motivated? How do you motivate your staff?
Loving what you do is the key to finding motivation each day. Love and respect from my housekeeping team is a huge motivating factor. The fact that I can make a small difference in the lives or experiences of our guests has kept me going in this industry for the last four decades.

I try to motivate the team by trying to instill the same value system in them. I also follow a people-oriented approach in dealing with the staff. Each employee has a different motivational trigger, and I try to understand and identify that. Having the team's trust and backing them through thick and thin is key to having motivated team members.

What are some ways you've looked to educate yourself and grow in your career?
I was certified by the American Institute of Lodging as a Certified Hospitality Housekeeping Executive (CHHE) in 2002 and continue to attend educational seminars and events to maintain that designation Further, I also completed my Hospitality Management certification in 2015. I completed the four-year online course within a year with a score above 90 percent.

With my acquired knowledge, I wanted to give back. I was able to inspire the young workforce to continuously upgrade their knowledge and skills to be in line with industry expectations and demands. I was subsequently awarded the Lamp of Knowledge Award in recognition of my contribution in sharing my experiences and mentoring young individuals within the industry by American Hotel & Lodging Educational Institute (AHLEI).

Can you tell us what it's been like for you as a woman in business?
In the early stages of my career, I had to deal with an inherently patriarchal society where the abilities and competence of a woman were always in question. A woman has to work harder and perform a lot better to be accepted as a leader and for her views to be respected and accepted by colleagues.

It's a lot better these days with women excelling in every field within the industry, but there is still a glass ceiling and resistance for women to reach the very top—especially at the board level. Very few women find representation at the very top of the industry.

The big challenge for any woman is to balance her personal and professional life. Family and motherhood demand as much time and attention as her professional career. Women play multiple roles at the same time and guilt can likely play a role in any working woman's life due to a feeling of "not being there enough." The key to success lies in finding a balance and having a supportive ecosystem of family, friends and colleagues.

How do you relax?
I'm an avid traveler. Traveling helps me take my mind off work for a couple of weeks each year. I also practice meditation, breathing exercises and yoga each day as part of my exercise routine. I feel that helps a lot with the stress management as well.

Are there a lot of women in roles similar to yours throughout the Middle East?
The numbers are definitely growing. The Middle East with its young demographics is undergoing a tourism boom. Dubai especially has invested a lot to emerge as one of the premier tourist destinations in the region and the world. There are tremendous opportunities for young women in the industry today and over the next decade. I would really like to see young women take up leadership positions in the industry, especially running the boards of the larger hotel groups, over the next few years.

What advice would you give to other women who are looking to advance their careers in the housekeeping industry?
Don't let anyone tell you it's not for you. Take up tough assignments, challenge yourself and never give in. You only lose when you quit. Women sometimes hesitate to take risks, speak out or take a stand. My advice to them would be to take risks and follow their instincts.

Sally

Schopmeyer

Sally Schopmeyer started at Maintenance, Inc., at the front desk, almost 30 years ago. Today, she's the president and has a minority interest in the company, and she also leads several of its subsidiaries. This mother of three shares how creative problem solving and her signature "pick me" approach have enabled her to get ahead in her career.

Name:
Sally Schopmeyer

Title:
President

Company:
Maintenance, Inc.

Location:
Dallas, Texas

Where Maintenance, Inc. & Subsidiaries Operate:
Arkansas, California, Colorado, Texas and Florida

About the Company:
For more than 40 years, Maintenance, Inc. & Subsidiaries has provided the finest in personalized, professional cleaning while serving as stewards for it's clients' janitorial dollars. It is recognized in the industry as an innovative leader for establishing safety programs for its employers and tenants, receiving BSCAI's Safety Award in the large company category several times.

Advice to Other People Looking to Advance in Their Careers:
Don't be afraid to delegate responsibilities. You need to build a team of people who are better than you in any given area.

Where You Can Find Her on the Weekends:
These days, you can typically find Sally on the sidelines of a soccer field, cheering on one of her three children.

> "You need to build a team of people who are better than you in specific areas. If you're constantly worried about your business, you don't have a strong enough team in place."

Tasked with "securing all existing accounts" when a long-term manager left a subsidiary of Maintenance, Inc. for a competitor, Sally opened the door to the client and introduced herself.

"Hi, my name is Sally Brucks and I'm your new account representative for Maintenance, Inc."

The man behind the desk smiled, standing to shake her hand.

"You mean you're not here for the Miss Texas pageant?" he asked, rhetorically, in a slow Southern drawl.

Sally forced a smile through her clenched teeth. It was one of the rudest things anyone had ever said to her before, a direct attempt to marginalize her and the existing contract. She refused to let him see just how angry she was.

"Oh, you're so funny!" she responded, feigning enthusiasm. "No, I'm not here for the Miss Texas pageant. As I was saying, your former contact, Tom, isn't with us any longer and I'm here to reassure you that we're extremely committed to your business and this territory."

He fired them a week later.

Sally Schopmeyer is president of Maintenance, Inc., a large building service contractor based in Dallas, Texas. She says that when she started in the business almost 30 years ago, she experienced challenges as a woman in a predominately male industry, but she worked past them, refusing to see the challenges as obstacles. Now, because of her experience and the increased prevalence of women at various levels in the industry, she doesn't feel the barriers at all.

"I think it's an asset being a woman in this industry," she said. "As long as you know the business, you work hard and you're tough when you need to be tough, there are no limitations on what you can accomplish."

Sally is a living testament to how hard work can get you ahead. A native of Dallas, after a few years of college Sally was working in the oil and gas industry, but the market was down so she accepted a job working for Maintenance, Inc.

"It was the lowest paying and least prestigious job I was offered, but everyone seemed happy, so I went with it," she said. "It turned out to be a very good decision."

In the 27 years that she's been at Maintenance, Inc., Sally has held a variety of positions. She's cleaned buildings during start-ups. She's worked in sales, marketing, human resources and operations. A product of a corporate culture that supports self-starters and people who want to get ahead, in her last 17 years as president, Sally has looked for ways to help other motivated performers advance in their careers.

Bill Travis, the company founder, recognized Sally's potential early on and took her under his wing. A structural engineer, Bill received his MBA from Harvard and successfully took two other businesses public before starting Maintenance, Inc. He also taught finance classes at Southern Methodist University in Dallas.

Sally credits him with being an incredible mentor, teaching her everything she needed to know about the business operations.

"I didn't have a formal education, but I received an incredible education from him," she said. "I remember a time when Bill, on a Friday afternoon, put a set of financials on my desk. He said he was considering an acquisition and would like me to review the documents and tell him on Monday if would be a good decision to acquire. Sally contacted her friends who were accountants and pored over the documents. She was ready Monday morning with pros and cons of the company and supporting data. That type of empowerment is ingrained in Sally and she manages with the same philosophy.

She says her early days in the business were an exciting time, as there were significant local market challenges, including an out-of-control Texas Workers Compensation system and a banking industry that no longer would accept service receivables for collateral, and

partners leaving the industry because it was such an impossible situation. Once one issue was resolved, another issue would appear—and where many people would tire from the stress, Sally found the creative problem-solving to be invigorating.

"I learned so much during that time—there was just problem after problem," she said. "I think that helped prepare me for when I was running the business more independently and the recession hit in 2007/2008. We made it through that period with increased profitability because strategically, I didn't wait for customers to go out for bid. We reviewed each account and proactively approached customers with reductions in cost (and scope of work) and have grown every year since. We came out stronger." To this day, she views challenges with excitement and as an opportunity to look for innovative ways to problem-solve. It's just one of several skills she's found to be essential for effective leadership.

"When the Affordable Care Act came in, I knew it was a game-changer and I had to read every article, document and opinion. I attended about 50 seminars on the subject," she said. "It was exciting to think how we could handle it and approach it so we can stay in business and come out ahead. Business is the art of correcting errors, and every time you're faced with an obstacle, there's a solution. You just need to find it."

Another critical skill that has helped Sally to get through tough times is the ability to be decisive. She says leaders who are paralyzed with fear and are unable to make quick and clear decisions won't be successful. An effective leader needs to work with his or her team to identify the problem, develop a solution and work collectively to enact that solution.

BUILDING A STRONG CORPORATE CULTURE

In the competitive world of contract cleaning, Sally seeks to differentiate their business and engage her team by building a strong corporate culture. Because their people are key to Maintenance, Inc.'s growth and success, Sally carefully considers all hiring decisions to make sure candidates are a fit with their corporate culture.

As the custodial work can be rigorous but also requires someone with customer service skills, she looks to employ individuals who have managed people in other similar industries, such as exterior landscaping or foodservice. She's found that hiring people who don't have experience specific to the cleaning industry brings a fresh perspective to the business and makes training easier.

"When you get people who have worked in the business, they think they already know how to do things," she said. "Many times, they're already burned out, which is why they want to switch companies. It might appear to be a quick fix but rarely does it work in the long term."

In addition to hiring the right people, Sally tries to reduce obstacles that limit her team's creativity and ideas. She wants to empower her team so they regularly contribute ideas that improve the overall culture.

"Our tenured executive management team is incredibly effective and motivated," she said. "It's a culture. And if you don't know what your culture is, you're in trouble. You have to have a culture your team believes in."

She backs up her culture-first approach by finding clients who want a premium cleaning service and realize there is a cost associated with it. That cost is never the lowest bid. The result is longstanding relationships that create value for both parties.

"We're not going to put our energy toward an account where someone is constantly looking for ways to cut costs," she said. "We want our managers to be in a quality account where they have enough labor to perform the work. We're not asking them to do the impossible. Churning business is not our culture and is not how we operate."

KEYS TO WORKING MOTHERHOOD

Sally and her husband, a criminal defense attorney, have three children who are each less than two years apart. Sally said she's a "freak of nature" who loved being pregnant.

"I sold incredible amounts of work when I was pregnant," she said, laughing. "I had to have a note from my doctor because I was traveling at eight and a half months pregnant and closing significant deals."

When the second and third child arrived, however, circumstances at home were a little more stressful. Sally's husband worked during the day as a public defender and was attending school in the evening to pursue an Electrical Engineering degree. Sally had just become president of Maintenance, Inc. and was traveling extensively. And while she says it was tough when the kids were younger, they were able to persevere with assistance from childcare providers and help from other parents. Sally and her husband spend a lot of quality time with their kids—often on the sidelines of the soccer field. But for Sally, being present for her children doesn't mean that she can't take a short work-related call.

"My kids understand that mom works, and that mom's work is important," she said. "They respect that."

Her home, office and children's school are all within less than 10 minutes of each other, an arrangement which was by design. Sally strongly feels that limiting commute time enables her to be very present in each aspect.

"There's no such thing as a work/life balance anymore," she said. "And that's okay. Some of my best friends are my customers and my co-workers."

When she does disconnect from work, she's able to do so because she's built such a strong team in whom she has full confidence to make decisions.

"I think a big mistake a lot of women make is that they don't delegate well," Sally said. "You need to build a team of people who are better than you in specific areas. If you're constantly worried about your business, you don't have a strong enough team in place."

TOOLS OF AN EFFECTIVE LEADER

Several years ago, her mentor and the company founder, Bill Travis, told her that if she wanted to be an effective leader, "everyone has to like you." And while Sally leads with congeniality, she's still firm and doesn't back down from confrontation when an issue arises.

"Confrontation is necessary," she said. "You can't run a company if you can't handle confrontation, in my mind. I never really have backed down from confrontation, and maybe that's from my experiences playing sports as a child. You just deal with it."

Another attribute Sally suggests to other women who are getting started in their career is to never compromise your integrity. The shortcuts may look appealing, but taking the easy route will ultimately undermine you and your culture in the long run.

Lastly, she suggests always looking for ways to improve your personal value and the value you bring to the business. For Sally, she looks for ways to improve the value she brings to the business through networking opportunities. She's connected with organizations large and small through Building Service Contractors Association International (BSCAI), which has been a tremendous benefit.

"We're in a 'do it' business—everything has to be cleaned every night," she concluded. "If you want to work hard, you can make a life and a career in this industry. Don't over promise, don't over commit—if you do that, you can build a great business."

A great business, just like Maintenance, Inc.

Laurie Sewell

Embracing an authentic leadership style, Laurie Sewell steadily climbed the ranks at Servicon Systems, where she now serves as president of the company. Along the way, she became a mother and has since found a way to strike a rhythm between responsibilities associated with her career and motherhood. For Laurie, success is derived in the outcomes of her efforts, rather than the time that goes into each role.

Name:
Laurie Sewell

Title:
President and CEO, Servicon Systems

About Servicon Systems:
Servicon Systems, founded in 1973, is an integrated provider of sustainable janitorial and facilities maintenance solutions and supplies. It employs more than 1500 full-time team members. The company services more than 100+ million square feet daily for a multitude of private and public industries, including aerospace, high-tech, biotech, healthcare and refineries. With top security clearances and personnel with expertise in complex, critical environments, Servicon has built longstanding relationships with major national and international firms, and earned a reputation for sophisticated best practices. Servicon was named by the Los Angeles Business Journal as one of the "Best Places to Work."

Location:
Culver City, California

Laurie's Advice for Women Looking for Professional Advancement:
Do your homework. Work hard to understand the business from the ground up, and don't be afraid to start something on your own. Step up, but don't step on people on your way to success. Be kind, and treat every person with respect. Don't burn bridges: reach out to find mentors and relationships at every possible turn. Learn from every single interaction. Give your time and talents to people even when there is no immediate benefit to you or your organization. Don't limit yourself to traditional sources for networking; I have learned a lot from friends and contacts in entirely different businesses.

What She's Doing If She Has a Bad Day:
Walking around the office barefoot, drinking tea or petting the company dog.

She was young. She was confident. She wore a brightly colored suit as she strode through the aisles of men wearing grey, navy and black. It was the mid '90s and Laurie Sewell was walking the floor of her first ISSA/INTERCLEAN® trade show.

"One of these things is not like the other," she sang to herself, flashing back to her childhood watching Sesame Street. It only took a few minutes for her to realize there was a small percentage of females attending the convention, but she would later understand the importance of her attendance. At the time, she was administrating the supplies division of Servicon Systems, a facility management firm headquartered in Culver City, California.

During the convention, she met a vice president of an international paper company. As they spoke, she mentioned that their corporate offices weren't far from her home in California. He encouraged her to stop by sometime and say hello.

A few months later, she decided to take him up on his offer. She had lost a bid due to a pricing issue with that supplier and she wanted it corrected. It was a huge company and she was doubtful he would see her on such short notice, but decided to give it a shot anyway.

An hour later, as she left the building and walked back to her car, she was still somewhat incredulous. The executive had welcomed her into his office, listened to the situation and immediately begun work on a solution for her company. The exchange resulted in a longstanding partnership between their organizations that continues today.

"Too often we don't do something because we feel it's impolite to go up a level in leadership, or that we need to wait for an invitation to make something happen," she said. "But that day I realized I could go and talk to anyone on the corporate ladder, regardless of their title or the size of the company. It doesn't matter what my sex, age, size of my company or industry is—they're just people like me."

A HAPPY AND COMPETENT PROFESSIONAL

In Sheryl Sandberg's international best seller "Lean In," she writes, "We need more portrayals of women as competent professionals and happy mothers—or even happy professionals and competent mothers."

Laurie Sewell is the president and CEO of Servicon and a mother of two who takes both jobs very seriously. Servicon, where Laurie's worked for much of her career, is one of the largest independent custodial contracting companies in the U.S. She started in an entry-level position and steadily grew in the business, nurturing the company just as she has her two children who came along mid-way in her career.

It's a balance that many women struggle with, but one that Laurie has embraced with vigor. She feels that the rhythm she's struck between the roles is a result of the care and appreciation she has for the people around her—whether they are her employees, the friends and family who enabled her to successfully raise two kids while also pursuing her professional dreams, or her children. She puts people first.

Employees and clients both know that she is serious about her work and about the company meeting its goals. However, when meeting with her direct reports, she is as likely to ask them about the status of their personal goals and happiness outside of work as she is their work metrics. "It is critical to value and address the whole person, not just the work," she says.

BUILDING A CAREER AND A FAMILY FROM THE GROUND UP

Laurie didn't get to the top overnight. She actually started at the bottom in an entry-level position. After receiving her bachelor's degree, she moved to Southern California and started at Servicon as a payroll clerk.

The more she learned about Servicon's operations, the better she wanted to understand the science behind cleaning and the larger industry. She spent hours with various team members learning tasks like how to strip and wax floors, how to drive a forklift and understanding the process of manufacturing chemicals. When she saw opportunities to gain efficiencies or create new systems for improvement, she made suggestions to the leaders of Servicon Systems and they listened. At the same time, she was learning about the people and the culture of Servicon, creating a foundation of trust that allows her to connect today as the CEO.

Laurie also jumped feet first into networking early in her career, something she feels benefitted her later on when she had children. In her early 20s, she joined the board of the Southern California Sanitary Supply Association to learn more about the industry and she embraced leadership opportunities. Then she was appointed by Linda Silverman, one of her primary mentors, to the board of the Young Executives Society (YES) before joining ISSA's International Board of Directors.

"Before I had my children, I was able to get involved and participate in leadership levels of industry associations," she said. "I think that really benefitted me, because once I stepped away and focused on my kids when they were younger, people knew who I was and what I could do, and remembered that when I returned."

DIVERSITY ISN'T JUST
WHAT YOU CAN SEE

When you look at the current leadership team of Servicon Systems, you'll see a diverse group of people representing different cultures and genders. Laurie laughs when asked about it, saying that while she greatly values diversity, the individuals in place were hired because they were the most talented people for the job. She feels the true strength in their leadership team isn't just in what they represent visually, but in the different personalities and styles.

"Sometimes people talk about diversity and focus on all the things you can see, and yes, you need people who come from different places," she said. "But I also try to think about what you can't see, which are the different personalities and styles. These factors are independent of race, sexual orientation and sex. We have people on our team who process things, problem solve, and communicate differently."

She highlights the company CFO, Maritza Aguilar, who is more of a process- and detailed-oriented person, where Laurie is more high-level and just needs a few pieces of information to run with something.

"Together, we do great things," Laurie said. "We're able to still move quickly and she prevents me from running off a cliff that I didn't see!"

Charged with identifying ways to grow Servicon, Laurie sought out Stephen Ashkin, the "father of green cleaning" in the U.S. After hearing him speak at a YES conference, Laurie was convinced that Servicon could embrace green cleaning in order to differentiate itself from competition and set an example in which the company could be proud.

She recognized that cleaning with sustainability in mind would not only align with the company's values but provide a great competitive advantage in the market. She immersed herself in the subject, learning as many strategies for improving the sustainability of their operations as she could find. In addition to developing one of the industry's first green cleaning programs, she was also a stakeholder on the committees that authored GS-42 -Green Seal Environmental Standard for Cleaning Services and ISSA's CIMS GB Standard.

"Green cleaning was an opportunity to differentiate Servicon, but more importantly, as a mother, I want to leave our environment intact for my children," she said. "I recognized that [green cleaning] wasn't a trend, but the way we should be doing business ad infinitum."

It's this progressive approach and willingness to try new ideas, as exhibited by Servicon's founder and previous leadership, that

Laurie has continued since becoming president in 2006. In addition, its focus on the 1,500 employees who work in the business has become a primary differentiator in a business that might otherwise seem stagnant. Servicon's founder, Richard Mahdesian is exceptionally supportive of Laurie's approach and continues to be an advocate for women in leadership. His wife, Dr. Gloria Mahdesian, held a Ph.D. of Psychology and was very influential in encouraging Laurie to achieve her Masters degree in Organizational Development in 2000.

One example of their innovative approach to developing and engaging the workforce is a new state-of-the-art training facility that opened a few years ago, the Mahdesian Learning Center and Client Innovation Hub. The center is a laboratory for field-testing new practices and is also home to the Servicon Academy where Servicon employees receive training. In keeping with their focus on sustainability, the building is Culver City's first LEED-New Construction Platinum facility.

"It's an old industry, but we're not an old business," she said with pride. "We act like a high-tech company, in terms of how we develop our people, the way our office looks, how we have fun and communicate. This has had a tremendous impact on the way we are able to attract high-level talent."

Once Servicon attracts great talent, they stay. Servicon boasts one of the lowest turnover rates in the industry, which is due in large part to the culture. It's been named one of the Best Places to Work in Los Angeles by the Los Angeles Business Journal. High retention rates are also due to the openness and style of the leadership team.

"Authentic leadership is a big thing for me," said Laurie. "I don't believe in being two different people. If you talk to me when I am with my kids, in the office, at home—you will get the same person. And sometimes I think women, more so then men, get it in their heads that they need to act a certain way as a professional. And it's not necessarily their style or personality, but what they think the workplace expects. That doesn't allow them to grow as fast as they can because they're not comfortable showing who they are, people can sense that dissonance and it doesn't facilitate trust."

A HAPPY AND COMPETENT MOTHER

Like any new parent, everything changed for Laurie when she had children. An entirely new world opened up and she developed her own signature style for approaching the demands between home and work. The key, she said, is finding a rhythm between the responsibilities associated with each and looking at the outcomes of her efforts, rather than the time that goes into each role.

"Family is first, but work is an enabler. As result, I try to act with intention, flowing between the two," she said. "Truthfully, guilt does creep in, but it's the signal that I use to analyze how I am doing with the kids and the work. I ask myself, 'Are the kids doing well, are they happy and adjusted' and about work 'Am I hitting my goals, is my team happy and hitting their goals?'"

Where most women subconsciously deal with the guilt, Laurie makes it a priority to address it. If there is a problem, she acts on it before it becomes a much bigger problem. This personal metric system helps keep her in check and avoid situations where she might feel like she missed out on something.

"When I perform this personal audit and look at the results and the outcomes, I realize I'm doing okay. Thinking about it that way, rather than focusing on the number of hours I spend in each place, allows me to manage the guilt better."

Where a lot of successful career women with young children have the strong support of a spouse who helps out at home, Laurie has developed a strong network of women—her "village," which is comprised of her family, friends and people from her church. They help out with activities like transporting kids to and from school or social events, or attending field trips. In return, Laurie tries to help out on the weekends by taking kids out for an activity.

"That reciprocation is really important to me, so I would take their kids on a Saturday. Even though people love you and want to help, you need to give back."

When she's not working, she tries to spend every available moment with her kids. And when it comes to personal interests and fitting in the time to accomplish household activities like grocery shopping, she involves her children so she's able to spend time with them and get things done. As her children have gotten older, she's also involved them more with her work.

"I have to be creative with my time," she said, "so if I want to be involved in a cause, I make sure to volunteer in a way that allows me to spend time with my children. When I work out, my kids would workout with me. I try to make chores fun; for example, at the grocery store, I would give them the list and turn shopping into a scavenger hunt. I try not to engage with anything that would take me away from them during my free time, but I also involve them with my work. Like if I have a big pitch, I'll practice it in front of them. We've grown to enjoy it and it has enabled me to forge a unique connection with my kids."

A WORK IN PROGRESS

When asked about what she does in her free time, Laurie laughs. She's a planner, so it's rare she gets much time to do something outside of her responsibilities at work or home. But she's found that work is her hobby and she's happiest when she's checking items off her to-do list. If her kids offer to make her dinner though, you will most likely find her reading a business or parenting book. As a self-declared "work in progress," she is always looking for ways to learn and grow.

"Every step has contributed to getting me to where I am today, and I am still looking for the next lesson I'm going to learn," she said. "I feel I still have plenty of room to grow, and to help others improve and grow, too. Even as a CEO, I'm still learning, improving and being coached."

Ultimately, while Laurie Sewell maintains two very different roles, she feels that each has informed the other. That having children has helped her become a better manager, and that becoming a manager has helped her become a better parent.

For Laurie, rhythm is the soul of life. The balanced work and family rhythm she has achieved in her life exemplifies the way Sandberg hopes to see more women portrayed. Laurie Sewell is both a very happy and competent mother and a very happy and competent professional.

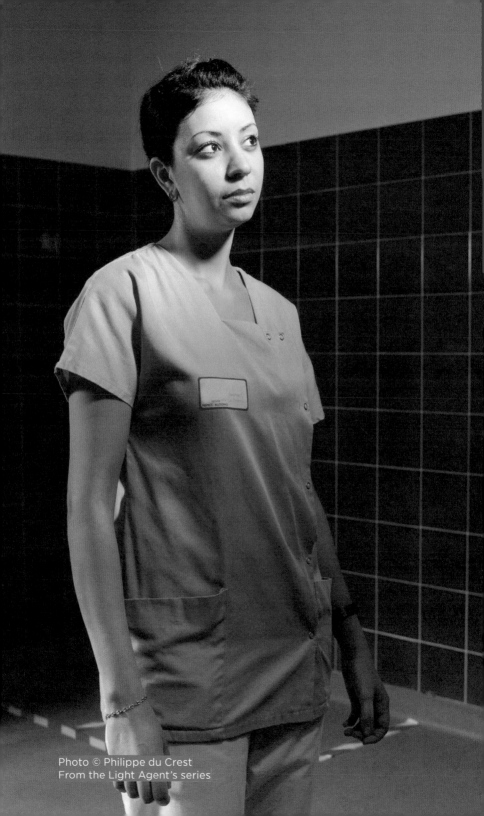

To Adrian, thanks for reading my story. Hope... Linda

Linda Silverman

In the late 70s, you didn't see many women selling janitorial supplies. Linda Silverman found that while her gender helped her get a foot in the door, the only way she would achieve success was through extensive preparation and a well-thought-out presentation. She now leads one of the largest distributorships on the west coast with her brother, Stu, and was the youngest female president in ISSA's 75-year history.

Name:
Linda Silverman

Title:
President, Maintex

Location:
Los Angeles, California

About Maintex:
Maintex is a chemical manufacturer and janitorial supply distributor. It manufactures more than 400 chemical formulations and sells several thousand facility cleaning supply items including cleaning equipment, paper, liners and cleaning tools. Maintex operates with an in-house direct sales team in Southern California and also private brands chemicals for other distributors throughout the Western U.S. Additionally, it sells items under the Maintex brand and private brand into big box stores and retailers nationwide.

Greatest Influence and Mentor:
Her father, Ralph Silverman, the founder of Maintex

Advice to Women Looking for Professional Advancement:
Find an organization where the culture fits and allows you to advance. Then you need to work hard, work smart, be prepared in all that you do. When it's presentation time, contribute your ideas in a direct and succinct manner.

"When I first started calling on customers, people were really surprised," Linda Silverman says of her early days as a salesperson for Maintex, a Los Angeles-based chemical manufacturer and distributor of janitorial supplies and equipment. "At that time, you didn't see women selling janitorial products, so I was somewhat of an enigma. I think that's why so many people agreed to take an appointment with me; they wanted to see who I was and what I was all about."

It was the late 1970s and Silverman had just joined the family business. A graduate of the University of California Los Angeles (UCLA), she had studied psychology and pursued that career for a few years before deciding to go in another direction. Her father had started Maintex in 1960 and she worked there during school breaks, but she never really entertained the family business as a career option. But after starting a house cleaning business with her college roommate and a short-lived stint in the travel industry, she found herself at a crossroads, and accepted her father's offer to try sales.

Almost immediately, she found success. While she'll be the first to say that her gender may have played a factor in setting the first appointment, it was her exhaustive preparation and research that helped her close the deal. Or, as she says it, "I did my homework."

"Most people at that time just didn't approach the sales process the way I did," she said. "I did my research and performed an analysis that sometimes required working my way into the back of the stores to see what products they were using and how they were using them. When I would go in for the presentation, I was ready. And that really wowed people."

In her first six months, she opened up several major grocery chains, school districts, and other retail establishments. She credits a mentor, Ray Gilmore, who took her under his wing and helped her understand the sales process and strategies for approaching the customer. He enabled her to see that the sales process wasn't about her, but the needs of the person standing in front of her.

"When I went into a meeting, my goal was to make the customer look good," she said. "And I think that still remains important today. If I was speaking to a grocer, I would tell them, 'You understand how to sell groceries, and we understand how to keep your floors looking bright and shiny and your facilities in sanitary conditions. Let me handle the floors so you can focus on your business.'"

DEVELOPING SUCCESSFUL MENTORSHIPS

One of the things that Silverman enjoys most about her career is watching other people succeed. She does this through mentorships.

With several successful mentorships under her belt, Silverman has found that the key to making a mentorship program work is having a good fit between the mentor and the mentoree. Before engaging in the relationship, she suggests defining expectations by asking questions such as:

- How much time will it require?

- What do you hope to achieve?

- How do you feel I can best help you?

Sometimes, Silverman says, the mentor doesn't always have to be the teacher. It can be about the mutual growth of both participants. She shares the story of a second-generation Asian businessman who was in a family business in a completely different industry. He'd initially asked to meet with her to discuss business, but through the relationship, she ended up learning much about his culture and industry.

The thing about Silverman was that she didn't just talk a good game. As she continued opening new customers and adding sales people to her team, she pushed herself to be better and to do more. Some might think that as the boss's daughter, she could have taken the easy route, but that wasn't her nature. She knew that if she wanted to have any credibility, she would have to prove herself.

"I had to look professional so people would listen to me. If you go into these meetings and you're waiting on someone to run the equipment or demonstrate the process for you, that diminishes your credibility."

To show people she knew what she was talking about, she mastered every cleaning process associated with the products she was selling. She stripped floors, ran burnishers and scrubbed railings. She was willing to work, and she worked proficiently.

"When my brother and I first started working for my father, he extended one of the best pieces of advice I've ever received. He told us that we were welcome in the business, but that we had to work harder and be better than anyone else. We both really took that information to heart. We try to lead by example. Even today I continue to work hard and give my best effort in all that I do."

GROWING THE FAMILY BUSINESS

After a few years in the business, the company saw great growth. Her brother, Stu, had joined Maintex just a few years before she started, and Linda says that the two worked well together. This enabled their father, Ralph Silverman, to return to the laboratory and focus on what he loved: chemistry.

"It was pretty amazing, really," Silverman recalls of her father's hands-off approach. "He gave us a lot of responsibility and authority. He never second-guessed any of our decisions."

She credits her father as having one of the biggest influences on her, both personally and professionally.

"He was the best person ever and always treated everyone equally," she continues. "That set the tone for us—how you talk to people and the way you treat them. It takes people to get things done, so you need to be fair and set expectations, but your employees need to take ownership in what they do for a business to operate at its best."

Linda and Stu continue to run the Maintex business as 50/50 partners—she oversees sales and marketing, customer service, research and development and the lab, and he handles all of the production and administrative activity such as accounting and legal.

"We work really well together," she said. "We are completely different people, but we both have the same goals and values. I think sharing the same values is what makes our relationship so successful."

BEING EFFECTIVE IN THE BOARD ROOM

As Maintex continued to grow, Linda became involved with other organizations to network and learn more about the industry. She served on the Board of the Southern California Sanitary Supply Association and participated in the Young Executives Society (YES), programs supported by ISSA, the worldwide cleaning association. The cleaning industry was still largely dominated by males at this time, so she had become accustomed to being the only woman in most meetings. But it never bothered her.

"When you're the only woman in the room, you might feel the urge to 'be like one of the guys,' but I never do that," she says. "You have to be who you are if you want to be heard."

That approach has helped her achieve much success. In the late 90s, Linda was elected to ISSA's national board of directors. She became the organization's second female president in 2000, and the youngest female to hold the position in its 75-year-history.

But achieving success and accomplishing goals in a male-dominated culture hasn't always come easily. Seeking to diversify the leadership in the cleaning industry, one of her goals as President of ISSA was to create a women's group.

The purpose of the group was to create channels for more women to become involved in the industry and offer networking and mentorship resources to help them advance in their careers. The idea was met with pushback from some other board members.

"ISSA was in support of it, but it was hard work to change some of the perceptions of the people who didn't feel the need to create something specifically for women," she says.

But using her systematic approach to research and planning, she lobbied for and successfully advanced the initiative in time. This women's group she started became the genesis of the women's forums still held during ISSA/INTERCLEAN's® annual conference and convention.

"One thing that I have learned is that to be effective in board meetings, you need to do the majority of the work before the meeting even happens," she advises. "Align the support you need by talking to other board members and help them understand what you're trying to accomplish. Anticipate what type of questions you may be asked or pushback you may receive. When you're prepared, you'll have a much better chance of accomplishing your goals."

BE PREPARED, SPEAK CONCISELY

The face of the cleaning industry has changed a lot since Silverman began, but she's learned a lot of techniques for becoming an effective leader and making change as she's charted her course. She hopes to see more women in executive leadership positions in the future and regularly mentors other women to help them advance in their careers.

When it comes to business, Silverman recommends the following:

DEFINE YOUR GOAL. Whether or not you're trying to sell a piece of equipment, raise money for a fund or get a "yes" vote for something you're trying to accomplish in the boardroom, define what it is you want to accomplish and work backward from that.

CONSIDER YOUR AUDIENCE. If you're talking to a group of retailers, there's a good chance they don't have a lot of time. Cut that presentation deck from thirty slides to five, and make sure you're talking about their business and pain points, not just about you and what you can do.

BE ORGANIZED AND SPEAK CONCISELY. She's observed women in advisory committees who have a tendency to ramble or make their points in an indirect or self-deprecating manner. This can result in being overlooked or not being heard at all. In contrast, a colleague makes the same point in a more definitive manner and is recognized for it. She suggests doing your research and coming to the table with all the information you need to make or support your objectives.

DON'T BE AFRAID TO TRY DIFFERENT THINGS.

She cites her experiences working for other business environments that helped her learn how to treat people and manage others. Sometimes you work in situations that are stressful and not optimal, but that will help you in the long run.

FIND ORGANIZATIONS THAT ARE SUPPORTIVE OF WOMEN.

Why fight an uphill battle? You will be most effective in a culture that is open to your ideas and shows a history of advancing women.

CLEARING A PATH FOR WOMEN IN CLEANING

Every industry has a trailblazer who helps chart the course for other women. In the cleaning industry, it's Linda Silverman. Only recently did she marry her partner of many years, but opted not to have children and focused largely on her career.

While maintaining a work/life balance is important to her, Linda Silverman focuses on defying expectations. She's accomplished this as a salesperson presenting to potential customers, as a solutions provider to facilities, as a female business leader, as a representative of the cleaning

industry and, undoubtedly, as a sister and daughter. She shows that having a seat at the table isn't enough. That through thorough preparation and by being yourself, you can accomplish whatever you want.

Hao Dang

Tanascos

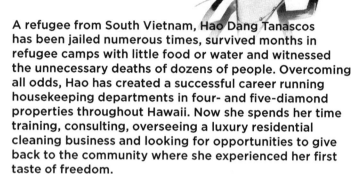

A refugee from South Vietnam, Hao Dang Tanascos has been jailed numerous times, survived months in refugee camps with little food or water and witnessed the unnecessary deaths of dozens of people. Overcoming all odds, Hao has created a successful career running housekeeping departments in four- and five-diamond properties throughout Hawaii. Now she spends her time training, consulting, overseeing a luxury residential cleaning business and looking for opportunities to give back to the community where she experienced her first taste of freedom.

Name:
Hao Dang Tanacsos

Title:
President

Years in the Housekeeping Industry:
31

Employer:
HAOskeeping Inc.

Location:
Island of Hawaii

Why She Chose this Profession:
As an immigrant to the U.S., Hao is committed to helping others like her. She feels the housekeeping department is a great place to meet new immigrants and provide them with pathways for growth and development. She also loves the challenges associated with housekeeping.
"Each day is like putting a puzzle together," she said.

Her Favorite Motivational Song:
"Imagine" by The Beatles

What She's Reading:
"Extreme You" by Sara Robb O'Hagan

One of Her Proudest Achievements:
Anytime she's mentoring staff or an assistant and sees them go on to become an executive housekeeper or general manager.

Inspirational Quote:
"Nothing is impossible, just impossible right now."

Favorite Thing to Do When She's Not Working:
Hao enjoys reading and cooking Hungarian and Chinese food.

Favorite Dish:
It depends on the regional cuisine she's preparing, but Hungarian Chicken and Vietnamese Chicken Curry are two of her favorites.

Conditions in the refugee camps were an improvement over her home in war-torn South Vietnam.

When Hao *(pronounced "how")* Dang Tanascos arrived in Hawaii, all she could think about was how amazing a single bite of a doughnut would taste. She'd spent the past several months living in refugee camps with her brother and had very little to eat. One day, she watched almost deliriously as a guard outside her tent enjoyed a doughnut. "If I could just have one bite," she thought, "I would not mind if I died right now."

Conditions in the refugee camps were an improvement over her home in war-torn South Vietnam. The North Vietnamese army had taken over her country and communism was the way of the land. As children, the atrocities of war were a way of life for Hao and her four brothers and sisters. But after awhile, it became too much. Despite the fact that their father owned one of the largest ice cream factories in the country, they had to leave the country if they wanted to guarantee their safety.

At first, the goal was just to escape. The children didn't know where they would eventually land, but simply wanted to find freedom. They had an aunt who lived in Hawaii and shared stories of the beautiful beaches, kind people and climate that wasn't much different from Vietnam. It was a vision that kept Hao and one of her brothers going through each of their seven increasingly dangerous attempts to escape.

Hao recalls the sixth attempt, which was the most traumatic. She sat sandwiched among several other refugees who were hidden in the hull of a boat when it came to a sudden stop. The propeller had become entangled in a fishnet. A guard boarded the boat and suggested that the captain remove some of the fish because the boat was too heavy.

When he realized that people were in the bottom of the boat, not fish, he began shooting indiscriminately along the hull. After he stopped shooting, they turned on the lights to arrest everyone. That's when Hao saw she was covered in the blood of a young boy who had been sitting next to her.

Hao's next attempt to escape was in 1980, a few years later. She hid once again in the hull of an overcrowded boat, packed with refugees. Once they sailed past Vietnamese waters, an atrocious storm hit and left them without a captain. Spotting a mountain in the distance, the group frantically paddled toward it—desperate for freedom, but reluctant to find what awaited them. When they finally stepped off the boat, they were arrested by Thai police. Two weeks later, they were released and sent to refugee camps.

When Hao finally arrived in Hawaii with her brother, she didn't have any money, nor did she speak any English. Her first job was taking orders at a Chinese restaurant during the day; in the evenings, she took language classes.

Her break into the cleaning industry happened when her aunt, a laundry attendant at a local hotel, notified her of an available housekeeping coordinator position. Potential candidates needed to be fluent in both Chinese and Vietnamese, two languages Hao spoke easily.

She applied for the job and was hired, thrilled because the management also agreed to work with her academic schedule. She had started taking courses in foodservice at a local community college and switched her concentration to hotel management when she realized how much she enjoyed interacting with different people in a hospitality environment.

Only eight months into her position as the housekeeping coordinator, the assistant executive housekeeper position became available. She had no intention of applying for it until the general manager approached her and promised that if she accepted the position, they would continue to accommodate her school schedule.

"School was my number one priority so I hadn't even really thought about the opportunity," she said. "But with such a flexible schedule, I thought it was too good of an offer to pass up!"

Hao had little practical experience in housekeeping, but dedicated herself to learning every responsibility performed by the people on her team. She worked alongside them, buffing and waxing floors, changing linens and disinfecting bathrooms, so she knew exactly what to do and how to do it. In addition to working directly with the housekeepers, she looked for every opportunity to gain knowledge about the industry. She participated in organizations like the International Executive Housekeepers Association (IEHA) where she served as the chapter president for two terms.

Throughout Hawaii, those who know Hao are quick to recognize her effervescent personality, enthusiasm and hard work ethic. Within the hospitality industry, she has earned a reputation for being a fair and effective manager. As a result, when she went on to help open several hotels on the island, including the Ritz-Carlton Mauna Lani and the Hapuna Beach Prince Hotel, she received a surprising number of applications for any opening she posted, despite the small local labor pool.

"They used to call me the Pied Piper," she said. "If I posted an opening in the newspaper, I'd get hundreds of phone calls. For example, when I opened the Ritz, I had almost 100 applicants and was able to hire 80 of them."

Her turnover rate also reflected her energetic, yet fair approach to management. As the director of housekeeping at the Mauna Kea Resort where she worked for more than 14 years, she maintained more than 85 percent of her original staff throughout her tenure. This includes staff members who drove more than 100 miles to come to work each day.

EMBRACING ENTREPRENEURSHIP

Hao's next position was at the Fairmont Kea Lani Maui, where she worked until the global economic downturn in 2009. The recession hit the hospitality industry particularly hard in the U.S., where room occupancy rates hovered just over 50 percent. To compete for travelers, hotels lowered their rates and as a result, were forced to consolidate and lay off employees.

Rather than compromise her signature level of quality and gold standard of cleanliness that would inevitably happen with the downturn, Hao saw a new opportunity emerge.

"I was excited," she said. "Hotels were consolidating and looking for people who could manage multiple properties. I thought it was a great time to quit my job and go into training and consulting."

Ready to be her own boss and have a little more flexibility with her work schedule, she made the jump into entrepreneurship. She admits that the decision was scary and filled with uncertainty, but she had been through a lot worse and knew that whatever happened, she would persevere.

Reaching out to recruiters, she found her first client. She trained a front desk manager who had been promoted to Executive Housekeeper, working alongside him to teach him the tricks of how to run a successful housekeeping department. But when that job was finished, Hao didn't receive another assignment for three months.

Finding that her connections to recruiters weren't delivering the desired results, she started reaching out directly to the 33 hotels on the island of Hawaii with a personal letter. Disappointingly, she didn't receive a single response.

"It's not a rainbow," she said of her experience starting her own business. But Hao refused to give up. And through her perseverance and professional network, she has launched a successful consulting career. She currently consults and trains for seven different properties.

To help offset the downtime between consulting assignments, Hao thought about her skills and how she could apply them to other areas. She approached local property management firms to see if she could assist with cleaning luxury homes they managed. They offered her a few trial properties as a start, and she has since grown her side venture into a successful business, HAOskeeping Inc., that now employs a small staff and has expanded to include cleaning personal jets.

She says her goal isn't to build a huge business, but she hopes to maintain her lifestyle and enjoy her leisure time.

"What's great is that I can pick and choose my clients," she said. "I can also make my own schedule, so if I have a friend coming to stay for a week, I can be flexible with when I work."

WEATHERING THE STORM

There are few who can tell such an inspiring tale of overcoming hardship and challenge as Hao. In addition to her consulting work and residential cleaning business, she also is an inspirational speaker. She regularly challenges others not to let a little pebble in your path become a roadblock to your success, but a stepping stone to your future.

For immigrants to the U.S. or another country, she says that one such road block might be a language barrier.

"When you live in a country where you can speak your native language, you don't have the same challenges of most immigrants," she said. "There are still times when I need to look up words. And when you come to a country after you are 15 years old or so, you will still have a thick accent. You want to speak perfect English, but sometimes people can't understand you. This makes you not confident."

To overcome this, she suggests completely immersing yourself in the local culture and finding ways to continue learning. She also recommends looking for employers who will help support your career goals, as her employer did many years ago.

And for custodial workers who have hit a ceiling in their career, she suggests looking around and thinking of how you can apply your skills somewhere else.

"The cleaning industry is so large and there's so much opportunity," she said. "Everything needs cleaned!"

But most importantly, the key to Hao's success is equal parts hard work and education. It's a formula she has proven more than once.

"When you give 100 percent all of the time, your work will be recognized. People will want you," she said. "Knowledge is key, but hard work is equally important."

Sherry Weavers

Sherry Weavers didn't know anything about the residential cleaning industry when she started Three Little Birds Residential Cleaning in 2012. She'd spent the past 12 years as a stay-at-home-mom, raising her three children, with her husband as the primary income earner. But that all changed in 2011 when she was diagnosed with breast cancer at the age of 41.Needing money for growing expenses, this self-described "control and order freak" was forced to let go and walk through the doors that opened for her as she entered a new and exciting chapter in her life.

Name:
Sherry Weavers

Title:
Owner

Company:
Three Little Birds Residential
Cleaning

Location:
Hamilton, Ontario

No. of Employees
She Oversees:
30

How Many Years She's
Been in the Business:
5

Who She Wants to Hire:
People who want to work to
live. Not the other way around.

> "I didn't realize people could be that way in business, and I was just blown away, people were sharing ideas, offering support—the more I learned, the more it seemed to fit with what I wanted to do."

When the doctor delivered the news, Sherry broke down and cried. Huddled against her husband in her doctor's office, she looked at him through her tears and apologized. It was her second positive diagnosis, and she felt awful bringing this horrible disease back into their lives. She apologized to her doctor. She knew she hated delivering this news and felt terrible making her do it.

Sherry kept crying. She cried because she felt like she was letting everyone down, all the wonderful people who had rallied around her and helped her through her first diagnosis. She cried because she was worried about her children. They were older this time and had seen other family friends lose their battle to cancer in recent months. She cried because it was scary and because she didn't know what would happen.

As the shock of the doctor's words started to sink in, Sherry thought about the first time she'd received the news and all she'd achieved since then. She thought about how she'd worked so hard to create a future she could control and build a better life for her family. She thought about the business she'd built and the amazing people who were working there.

When she thought about that, she realized it would be okay, and that everything would be taken care of. She knew that everything would be all right.

While breast cancer is the most common cancer of females across the globe, most women don't think it will happen to them. Until it does. This was the case for Sherry Weavers of Hamilton, Ontario. In 2011, hers was one of the 1.7 million new cases of breast cancer diagnosed worldwide each year. She was only 41 when she received the news the first time—around the age when doctors recommend women consider their first mammogram screening. And like so many other cancer patients, the diagnosis changed everything for her.

For the previous 12 years, Sherry had dedicated herself to raising the family's three young children. She said she couldn't imagine missing a soccer practice or school event—it was a decision that was right for her. But the events of 2011 were a perfect storm that made her rethink her options and next career steps. The family car was in disrepair, updates were needed around the house—and to top it all off, Sherry now learned that she had breast cancer.

"We were tapped," she said. "Things were going south and all I could think about was how we could make things work. And then I realized I just needed to give up, go with the flow and have faith that everything would work out. And it did."

From an early age, Sherry wanted to start her own business, but she was never sure what she should do. After the diagnosis, she realized that now was the time to act. She researched business options, stumbling upon a small residential cleaning association. The online group was extremely welcoming and supportive, filled with people sharing strategies they'd learned along the way to become successful in the residential cleaning business.

"I didn't realize people could be that way in business, and I was just blown away," she said. "People were sharing ideas, offering support—the more I learned, the more it seemed to fit with what I wanted to do."

Refusing to let the treatments hold her back, Sherry began building her business from the ground up. She found online business building resources, including a complementary website and domain hosting service. Through the association, she also met another local woman who only used natural cleaning products in her residential cleaning business and offered to take her under her wing—an approach Sherry had decided would best align with her mission and values.

From there, Three Little Birds Residential Cleaning was born. Sherry chose the name to represent her three children, and to pay homage to the Bob Marley song, "Three Little Birds," which offered her the continual reassurance that "every little thing gonna be alright."

A BUSINESS WITH A FAMILY FOCUS

Sherry admits that the jump into entrepreneurship was scary and challenging, but she felt reassured that she was in the right place with each step. Her mother worked alongside her in the early days, concerned she was still too weak to work because of the radiation treatments. When Sherry experienced any issues, she leaned heavily on the relationships she'd formed with other business owners who helped her work through them.

"There were probably 100 times a day I felt like quitting," she recalled. "But I convinced myself that if I lasted just one more hour, I could get over the hump. And then one day, it happened. Things just became easier."

As the business grew, she developed policies and procedures along the way, giving careful thought to how she would want to be treated — both as an employee and as a customer. Because she would want to work in a business that values a commitment to family, she made that a guiding focus of her company's mission.

In addition to being a great business differentiator, the focus on family values enables TLB to attract employees and clients who respect hard work, integrity, family and cleanliness. TLB will not accept clients who are disrespectful to staff members or put them in an uncomfortable situation.

"We're very selective about the clients we choose to work with," she said. "It's always been our belief that it's easier to replace a client than a quality employee. "

Another key focus for the business has been an emphasis on "healthy" cleaning. TLB cleaners only use cleaning products that contain natural ingredients, such as water, hydrogen peroxide and essential oils. After receiving repeated requests from customers who commented on the wonderful smell in their homes after a cleaning, Sherry worked with her team and started packaging the products for retail sale in their office.

Uncovering the key factor in TLB's growth and success, however, requires only a quick glance at the people they've employed. When they market their company, TLB doesn't position itself as the cheapest home cleaning service around or talk about the "sparkle" they'll leave behind. They talk about the quality of their staff.

"Our clients know what a clean home looks like, so we don't talk about that," Sherry said. "We want them to feel comfortable with the people in their home and be confident that our team will provide excellent service. It's about the people."

CREATING AN EMPOWERING CULTURE

If you're applying for a job at Three Little Birds Residential Cleaning and list "love to clean" as a reason for applying, there's a good chance you won't get the job. That's because Sherry and her office managers, Sarah Hurst and Chantelle Gagne, aren't looking for a team of people who love to clean. They want to hire people who don't want to work in the evenings and weekends, and are willing to work in the cleaning business.

"There are a lot of 'trunk slammers' out there," Sherry said. "These are people who have a mop, a bucket and call it a cleaning business. But when they get sick or their car breaks down, there's no backup plan to make sure your house gets cleaned. Our goal is to build a business by making the company a happy place that attracts the best workers."

One way they attract a quality team is by offering great benefits and recognizing that people have lives and responsibilities beyond work. Sherry and her management team want employees to enjoy what they do, feel valued and not take any stress home with them. TLB offers two weeks paid vacation, set schedules, company-paid health and dental benefits after one year of employment, and a company policy that states that if school buses aren't running, the business isn't running.

"There shouldn't be anything stressful about cleaning someone's home," Sherry said.

"If someone has any issues, we ask that they direct them to the office. Our cleaners don't need to deal with that. Because of our approach, people with college degrees join our business. They may start their careers with other ambitions, but when they have kids, there are a lot of parents who want to be with their children. We want to give these people a flexible working solution so they can focus on their families."

Sherry and the management team promote an open-door policy that encourages transparency at all levels. They are very open about company sales, programs and issues with clients or staff members. In return, they encourage team members to share their challenges, dreams and future career ambitions. An upcoming initiative is for team members to create individual "dream boards" where they can post personal and professional goals.

"For a lot of our staff, this is just a stepping stone in their career and we realize they won't be with us forever," she said. "But we're always looking for ways we can help our staff grow while they are with us."

Low employee turnover has been an unexpected dividend of the company's "employees first" approach. But it wasn't until Sherry talked to industry peers at her first Association of Residential Cleaning Services International (ARCSI) convention that she realized TLB's approach was unique. The 30 employees on staff have formed a tight-knit group, supporting each other through the ups and downs of life.

"One of our employees recently left an unhealthy relationship and it's been incredible to watch our team rally around her," Sherry said. "Other staff brought in paint, furniture and decor for her new apartment, and helped clean it before she moved in. No one gets left behind and to me, that's what it's all about. That's living life. I love seeing and enabling that kind of environment."

A FAMILY AFFAIR

In 2016, Sherry was notified that her cancer had returned. But when she needed to step out of the business for six months for treatment, work was the last thing on her mind. She knew she had an extremely competent team who would keep things running in her absence.

"After the diagnosis, I had a full mastectomy and reconstruction surgery," she said. "I just stepped away and the staff just took over. It was really something to see that the organization could run without me, and just how caring and supportive our team was."

Now that she's back and cancer-free, Sherry and her team have plans to triple business with little change to the company structure beyond adding personnel. She said that the biggest motivation for growth is the need for developing new positions and opportunities for staff members so they don't lose them. In the next few years, TLB hopes to add a new location that will be led by existing staff members who have been promoted to new positions.

She looks to her husband, a trained marketer, for guidance in developing programs to build awareness for the business, but more recently she's also found creative ways to engage her children in helping build the business.

For example, when her oldest son turned 16, he bought a car. To help him make the payment, Sherry worked out an arrangement with him that if he'd agree to driving around with a wrap on his car promoting the company, TLB would compensate him.

"Our company logo has a big baby reaching for a leaf," she said. "So, my 16-year-old son drives a car to school with a giant baby on it. The image is great, but it's an effective way to teach our kids about business and give back."

She's also engaged her middle son, who is skilled in graphic design, to assist with the development of the company's marketing collateral and advertising campaigns.

"It's absolutely amazing," she said. "When you're thankful for the staff, we continue to get more wonderful staff. When you're thankful for great clients, we continue to get more wonderful clients. And even thankful when we know we're being taken advantage of—because we know, if you do the right thing, good will come back to you."

It's just like Bob Marley crooned. "Every little thing" for Sherry Weavers and the team at Three Little Birds Residential Cleaning, is "gonna be alright." All right, indeed.

THE POWER OF APPRECIATION

Since her original diagnosis in 2011, Sherry has taken a life-shaking challenge and turned it around into a tremendous opportunity. She credits a strong faith in God for her ability to persevere through the tough times, but also a firm belief that a "thankful" approach helps attract more good.

Lydia Work

Name: Lydia Work
Title: President and CEO
Company: American Paper

"The only obstacle to achieving your goals is allowing what you do not want to do stop you."

What advice would you give to other women who are looking to advance their careers in the cleaning industry?
Do not think about being a woman in business, think about being a leader in business.

BACKGROUND AND GOAL SETTING

Lydia Work is a native of Nicaragua. After graduation from high school her strong desire was to be a chemical engineer.
The English language was not only not her strength, she did not actually have an interest in the language. So she realized in order to accomplish her goal she had to overcome that feeling and learn the English language.

PURSUING GOALS

She decided to come to the USA as an exchange student to learn English. Shortly after her arrival a massive earthquake in Nicaragua forced her to stay in the USA longer. For weeks she did not know if her family had survived or not. Her family lost their entire business during the earthquake. This made it financially difficult to pursue a college education in the United States for Lydia. Her host family asked her what she desired to be. She replied, a graduate in chemical engineering from an American university. But, she added, this is like asking if I want to be the president of the USA, which is impossible.

MAKE IT HAPPEN

Later that evening Lydia gave it further thought and decided that money was not going to be the obstacle to achieving her goals. So, she started to pursue all avenues. She went to the immigration office to obtain a work permit which she knew was very difficult to obtain. The immigration officer commented during the interview, that he had heard on the news on his way to work that morning that Nicaragua had another massive earthquake and he then proceeded to grant her the work permit. With this permit, she was allowed to work for the university, pay in-state-tuition, and earn money to pay for the schooling. During her last year of study, she earned a scholarship from the university that paid for her schooling.

She had accomplished her goal - a graduate from the University of Washington with a degree in Chemical Engineering. After graduation, she worked in the pulp and paper industry and later embarked on creating her own company. She had worked for several major integrated paper mills and gained experience in newsprint, linerboard, and towel/tissue manufacturing and converting.

TAKING THE BIGGEST CHALLENGE - FOUNDING A COMPANY

In 1997, she founded American Paper Converting Inc. (APC), a manufacturer of towel and tissue products for the away from home market where she applied her strong drive for innovation and sustainability. She is currently the President and CEO. APC's goal has been to support independent distributors with innovative and differentiated products. During the past 20 years APC has used experience, not grand designs, to grow from zero to over one hundred employees nationally with manufacturing locations in Woodland, WA and Richmond, VA. The current capacity supports markets across the entire U.S. as well as Central America.

LYDIA'S PRINCIPLES

SUSTAINABILITY.
APC was founded with a simple goal; to support a healthier earth with the use of environmentally friendly products and give back to the communities we serve.

INNOVATION AND DIFFERENTIATION.
APC creates customized recycled products backed by sales to independent distributors. The organization's growth is a result of its commitment to outstanding customer service and creative solutions to deliver the product on time, meet/exceed quality expectations, and provide innovative products at a competitive price.

SERVING OUR COMMUNITY AND OUR INDUSTRY.
Sponsoring women and small business and seeing them succeed has been her involvement and commitment. In 2012, Lydia was elected to serve as the President of the International Sanitary Supply Association. This position broadened her experience in the industry and was very rewarding both personally and professionally.

THE KEY TO SUCCESS, THE TEAM.
Our customers, employees and vendors, are all key. APC is driven by challenges and commitment to customers, resulting in growth opportunities for its customers, business and employees. APC motivates their employees by valuing an open creative work environment and focusing on ethical business practice. Employees are rewarded for their creativity.

THE DRIVING FORCE FOR SUCCESS.
The only obstacle to achieving your goals is allowing what you do not want to do stop you. Perseverance and determination can overcome any obstacle.

The striking images of cleaners shown in this book are the work of acclaimed French photographer
Philippe du Crest

Born in 1959 in Marseille, where he lives and works.

Self-taught artist? Even if that was what people said about my beginnings in photography, I prefer the idea of a life traveller; following a professional road which drove me – thanks to meeting people, from experiences about production and image manipulation – to a job as a photographer.

Since that moment, I have worked on several series in a connected way with an endless subject: the human condition.

In that way, when I photograph a series of cleaner's portraits at their work place; when I push the door of operating rooms in La Cella Moderne; when I "dive" naked models in the back of limestone landscapes, or when I meet some people concerned by the gender question for the Trans' Humanités project - humanity in all its dimensions seems to be at the heart of the process.

Photos © Philippe du Crest
From the Light Agent's series

Philippe Du Crest's Achievements

EXHIBITIONS

2018 – La Cella Moderne International Biennale of pictures, Nancy

2016 / 2017 – Projection - La Cella Moderne Photographie
présences - Montélimar

2016 – Collective exhibition - La Cella Moderne - Voices over -
Arles

2016 – Exhibition - Light Agents - Community of Caen
agglomeration

2016 – Exhibition - Light Agents - Tours Town Hall

2016 – 1st Prize Rendez-vous Pictures - Strasbourg

2015 – Relief – Triptyque Gallery - Marseille

2015 – Selection of twenty winning images for Life Framer 11: The
Human Body, pictures take from La Cella Moderne

2015 – Jury special prize at Les nuits photographiques of
Pierrevert – 31 July, 1&2 August 2015

2015 – Relief – Pullman Hostel - Marseille

2015 – ART'UP, Trade show of contemporary art - Lille

2014 – ST'ART, Trade show of contemporary art – Strasbourg

2014 – Exhibition - Jam Fusion - Sanilhac Castel – Sanilhac –
Sagriès

2013 - Exhibition - La Cella Moderne - Provences study – Marseille

2013 – Series - Relief

2012 – Series about transgender

2012 – Series - Light Agents

2008 – 2012 – Series La Cella Modern

AWARDS

2013 – Best photo prints – of 10,000 in the 2013 Palmares of
professional press

2015 – Jury special prize - Les nuits photographiques of Pierrevert
for La Cella Moderne

2016 – Selection for the Espace Beaurepair prize – Thérèse
Gutmann – Paris

PUBLICATION

2017 – NIEPCEBOOK 4 – La Cella Moderne

PHILIPPE DU CREST

The philosophy behind the Light Agents images

Emergence... Thirty portraits, thirty faces flaunted, thirty people who accept to show themselves; to arise from the shadows - to emerge under the light.

The exhibition's title, *Light Agents* was not chosen by Philippe du Crest by chance.

This series - which was started in 2011 by the photographer - was made in 2012 in Marseille, in companies and training centres.

The series is a telescoping of the photographer's life: the past with his grandmother who "cleaned houses" and the present - with his reading of the *Le Quai de Ouistreham* by Florence Aubenas, a book which recounts her experience as a cleaner.

With this title, the photographer invites people to watch these women and men who are not recognised, almost invisible; these people described as "workers of the shadow": those who work in the evening, in the night, or in the early hours as cleaning agents.

Each of them is shot in a ¾ frame at their work place, with their outfit and work tools in their hands following the traditional representation of professions that can be found in Nicolas de Lamerssin prints, or closer to us; on Eugène Atget's photography in the streets in Paris, from the late nineteenth and into the twentieth century.

The body is shown from the front or in a slight profile view, two flashes enlighten the face looking toward us, or that is inclined in a kind of daydream - illuminated by a smile. This singular attitude breaks with the usual representation of this profession: a Madonna facial expression for a young trainee, a depiction in an outfit with a mask like from his transgender series; nails perfectly manicured, with jewellery and makeup.

This portrait gallery seems similar to those from Studio Harcourt. The same serenity emerges, which seems almost out of time thanks to a specific lighting choice; what could be described as a beauty enhancement. As in seventeenth century Flemish painting, when the world was reflected in a housekeeper's pearl earring...

However, the colours give dynamism and vigour to the series of pictures and make it resolutely modern and rooted in the France of today.

This almost sociological procedure is reinforced by a common modus operandi for all the photos and by the voluntary presence in the background of either the work environment, or specific items relative to the profession.

Philippe du Crest makes very few colour and frame changes, because he thinks that the look of the photograph on his subject must be the most important element.

As Robert Capa said: "The beauty is there, and you just have to catch it". But this beauty must not overflow because the photographer is not in a disciplined aesthetic; he should channel his ideas in order to avoid getting away from his main goal and to delve more deeply in to that which is seen.

However in this series, Philippe du Crest assumes an influence more pictorial than photographic. Immersed in painting since childhood and with a painter mother, Philippe du Crest plays with the hot and cold opposition in a classical way. He highlights colour swatches in simple and purified compositions.

Vibrant colours are powerful and reinforced by his choice of a Photo Tecco Baryté print run, which stresses contrast and detail. The detail which is so important for Philippe, like a strong presence of the hands which symbolise the soul of the worker.

On another hand, the stark light in some part of the composition creates a halo effect which boosts the concentrated colours. No halftone, but solar classicism! The same as the photographer with his open attitude, his energy to meet the other in an unexpected way. With his choice of a frontal composition, he make us enter the picture immediately.

His eye is watching, then reading and framing. The principle of a series gives a coherence to the photographer's procedure. He has already used the same series method in the past with *La Cella Moderne*, which took place in operating rooms, hospitals and clinics between 2008 and 2016. He used the same humanist approach: a work place, people in the shadow, precise gestures, targeted light; impressions chiaroscuro inspired by *Le Caravage*.

In this series, the apprehension of Philippe du Crest is felt, his senses are awakened and reveal what we don't know, or what we don't want to know - something unreachable.

Humanity can be read in the series *Light Agents* because the photographer knows how to give his model confidence; to push them into revealing a positive energy and display a pride that was maybe forgotten. In our society where the values of work are often dismissed, he makes them noble again.

Photography, which is a common medium, seems to be the best way to show something different, something inconvenient, hidden or inappropriate; in order to ask ourselves about our failures and our own vision of life - all thanks to our response to this particular aesthetic.